THE PSYCHOLOGY OF DREAMING

Why do we dream? What is the connection between our dreams and our mental health? Can we teach ourselves to have lucid dreams?

The Psychology of Dreaming delves into the last 100 years of dream research to provide a thought-provoking introduction to what happens in our minds when we sleep. It looks at the role that dreaming plays in memory, problem-solving, and processing emotions, examines how trauma affects dreaming, and explores how we can use our dreams to understand ourselves better.

Exploring extraordinary experiences like lucid dreaming, precognitive dreams, and sleep paralysis nightmares, alongside cutting-edge questions like whether it will ever be possible for androids to dream, *The Psychology of Dreaming* reveals some of the most fascinating aspects of our dreaming world.

Josie Malinowski is Lecturer in Psychology at the University of East London, UK, who specialises in dream research. Her research on dreaming has been featured in *TIME* magazine, *The Guardian*, and *The Independent*.

THE PSYCHOLOGY OF EVERYTHING

People are fascinated by psychology, and what makes humans tick. Why do we think and behave the way we do? We've all met armchair psychologists claiming to have the answers, and people that ask if psychologists can tell what they're thinking. The Psychology of Everything is a series of books which debunk the popular myths and pseudo-science surrounding some of life's biggest questions.

The series explores the hidden psychological factors that drive us, from our subconscious desires and aversions, to our natural social instincts. Absorbing, informative, and always intriguing, each book is written by an expert in the field, examining how research-based knowledge compares with popular wisdom, and showing how psychology can truly enrich our understanding of modern life.

Applying a psychological lens to an array of topics and contemporary concerns – from sex, to fashion, to conspiracy theories – The Psychology of Everything will make you look at everything in a new way.

Titles in the series:

The Psychology of Vampires
David Cohen

The Psychology of Chess
Fernand Gobet

The Psychology of Music
Susan Hallam

The Psychology of Weather
Trevor Harley

The Psychology of Driving
Graham J. Hole

The Psychology of Retirement
Doreen Rosenthal and Susan M. Moore

The Psychology of School
Bullying
Peter Smith

The Psychology of Celebrity
Gayle Stever

The Psychology of Dog
Ownership
Craig Roberts and Theresa Barlow

The Psychology of Social
Media
Ciarán Mc Mahon

The Psychology of Happiness
Peter Warr

The Psychology of Politics
Barry Richards

The Psychology of the
Paranormal
David Groome

The Psychology of Prejudice
Richard Gross

The Psychology of
Intelligence
Sonja Falck

The Psychology of Terrorism
Neil Shortland

The Psychology of Dreaming
Josie Malinowski

The Psychology of Exercise
Josephine Perry

The Psychology of Video
Games
Celia Hodent

The Psychology of Religion
Vassilis Saroglou

The Psychology of Belonging
Kelly-Ann Allen

The Psychology of Art
George Mather

For further information about this series please visit www.routledge
textbooks.com/textbooks/thepsychologyofeverything/

THE PSYCHOLOGY
OF DREAMING

JOSIE MALINOWSKI

Routledge
Taylor & Francis Group

LONDON AND NEW YORK

First published 2021
by Routledge
2 Park Square, Milton Park, Abingdon, Oxon OX14 4RN

and by Routledge
52 Vanderbilt Avenue, New York, NY 10017

Routledge is an imprint of the Taylor & Francis Group, an informa business

© 2021 Josie Malinowski

The right of Josie Malinowski to be identified as author of this work
has been asserted by her in accordance with sections 77 and 78 of the
Copyright, Designs and Patents Act 1988.

British Library Cataloguing-in-Publication Data
A catalogue record for this book is available from the British Library

Library of Congress Cataloging-in-Publication Data
A catalog record for this book has been requested

ISBN: 978-1-138-69949-6 (hbk)
ISBN: 978-1-138-69951-9 (pbk)
ISBN: 978-1-315-51665-3 (ebk)

Typeset in Joanna
by Apex CoVantage, LLC

Dedicated to all the world's oneironauts

CONTENTS

ACKNOWLEDGEMENTS

I am extremely grateful to my fellow dream researchers and travellers, my family and friends, and the editorial team at Routledge for their contributions to this book coming together. In particular, my thanks go to Jason Abdelhadi, Carrie Addams, Mark Blagrove, James Cameron, Andy Cherry, Paul Cowdell, Paul "Moon Bear" Day, Nacho Díaz, Chris Edwards, Leslie Ellis, Saio Sofa Gradin, Clare Jonas, Lucy Kennedy, Robert Lindroth, Sue Llewellyn, Adam Malinowski, Carolyn Malinowski, Juan Carlos Otaño, Rachel Raider, Judy Schoßböck, and Emma Thomas for their careful readings and feedback on the manuscript. I'd also like to acknowledge the invaluable role the International Association for the Study of Dreams has played in bringing oneirologists together and providing us a place to obsess about dreams together. I've always been fascinated with dreams, but the joy with which I began to engage with them many years ago is thanks primarily to the members of the Surrealist London Action Group. Huge thanks also go to my long-time collaborator and friend, Caroline Horton, for steering me along in my oneirological explorations, and to all of my other collaborators. Finally, thank you to everyone who volunteered their time and their dreams, without whom none of this research would have been possible.

INTRODUCTION

DREAM LIFE

Dreams are true while they last, and do we not live in dreams?

The Higher Pantheism, Lord Alfred Tennyson

Dreams happen in our minds, spinning stories from our memories and our imaginations.

They are also real.

Dreams are often contrasted with 'real life', as if dreams somehow weren't part of real life. And yet we all dream every night.[1] These dreams are packed full of our anxieties, our fears, things of which we're in awe, things we expect to happen, things that have already happened, our loved ones, our wishes and desires, intense emotions, spectacular absurd humour, impossibly wonderful scenarios, terrifying ordeals that make us wake up in a cold sweat, eureka! moments of realisation, myths, stories, visual delights, and so on.

We might not be in the waking world, up and moving around, but try telling that to your dreaming body. The only reason it is not up and about is because we have evolved a neural mechanism – a part of the brain – that stops us from moving around during our most vivid forms of dreaming. We experience dreams as if they were 'really' happening in our brains, in our bodies, and in our minds. We live in them.

For this reason, dream psychologists prefer to contrast dreaming life with 'waking life', rather than with 'real life'. Both dreaming and waking lives are part of *real life*. Night life and day life: both as real as each other when we are in them.

In this book, we'll be delving into this nocturnal life and exploring what has been discovered about dreams in the discipline of psychology. Plenty has already been written about the early days of dream psychology, especially by Freud, Jung, and others who came from the psychoanalytical tradition, so although we'll cover them briefly, this book will focus more on what has been happening since then. It will present research that's innovative, exciting, and cutting-edge, and will try to answer the most intriguing and enigmatic questions about dreams.

In Chapter 1, we ask ourselves what actually *are* dreams? How do we define them, what types of dreams are there, and how do we research them?

Chapter 2 will take us on a whistle-stop tour of the history of dreams to see where we've been, where we are now, and where we will perhaps go next: from ancient dream interpreters, to 20th-century psychoanalysts, through to present-day cognitive neuroscientists.

In Chapter 3, we ask perhaps the biggest question of them all: *why* do we dream? In this chapter, we'll look at some of the main psychological theories that attempt to answer this question.

Dreams don't always serve us well, however, so in Chapter 4 we'll be looking at ways in which dreaming seems to 'go wrong': in particular, the nightmares that may follow traumatic experiences, and the link between dreaming and psychosis.

In Chapter 5, we ask another big question: what can we *do* with our dreams? We'll discover ways of exploring and working with our dreams that have been developed by psychotherapists and psychologists. This chapter includes suggestions for how to explore and experiment with your own dreams.

Chapter 6 takes us to some of the most extraordinary dreams: lucid dreams (dreams in which you know that you're dreaming), precognitive dreams (dreams that seem to predict the future), and sleep paralysis nightmares.

Finally, in Chapter 7 we project ourselves into the future and ask what dream research might look like next and how likely this is based on technology that is being developed now. Will the technology of sci-fi movies like *Inception* – in which ideas can be planted into a person's mind while dreaming – one day exist? Can dreams be 'hacked'? And when artificial intelligence develops further, will androids dream?

TERMINOLOGY

The study of dreams is called 'oneirology', coming from the Greek words 'oneiron' (dream) and 'logia' (the study of). Those who study dreams, therefore, are oneirologists. I will be using the terms 'oneirology', meaning dream research, and 'oneirologist', meaning dream researcher, throughout this book.

The book is accompanied by a website, www.oneirology.co.uk. If, during the course of your reading, you come up against a term that you haven't seen before, or it was defined earlier in the book and you've forgotten what it means, head over to the website. There you will find a 'Glossary of Dreamy Terms' in which definitions are provided for sleep/dream-related terms. The website also contains some extra details about the information in the book for those who would like to delve a little deeper.

A CAUTIONARY TALE

The research presented in this book mostly comes from the world of experimental psychology; it is research that uses the scientific method to investigate the phenomenon of dreaming. This is by no means the only way of researching dreams, but it is the current dominant paradigm in 'Western' dream psychology, and many fascinating things have been discovered with these methods, as you'll discover.

When reading the book, however, you may like to keep in mind that paradigms change over time. As we'll see briefly in Chapter 2, the way dreams are conceptualised, interpreted, and used is hugely dependent on where in the history of the human race you are and whereabouts in the world you are. At the moment, many oneirologists are investigating, exploring, and experimenting with dreams as psychologists, as opposed to, for example, priestesses, prophets, or psychoanalysts. The insights we have unearthed about dreams that you will read about in this book are an important piece of the dream-puzzle, but we have many more pieces of the puzzle yet to be found.

Be aware also that claims made in psychology about humans actually usually mean **WEIRD** humans: that is, research participants or volunteers tend to be **W**estern, **E**ducated, from **I**ndustrialised countries, from relatively **R**ich countries, and from (at least ostensibly) **D**emocratic countries – who are, when taken in consideration of the whole of human history and the whole of the human world, therefore, actually quite *weird* in the sense of not being representative of all humankind (Henrich et al., 2010). This is a discipline-wide problem – it is not just in dream psychology that this occurs – but it's something else to keep in mind: the research findings presented herein are often derived from data gathered from WEIRD participants.

1

WHAT ARE DREAMS, AND HOW DO WE STUDY THEM?

DEFINING THE DREAM

You might already have a pretty firm idea about what dreams are to you personally. But defining what a dream is (and is not) is not actually all that clear-cut. In oneirology, there are a few different definitions of 'dream' bouncing about. For the purposes of this book, we'll use a definition of dreaming that's commonly used in oneirology, which is 'all conscious[1] experiences during sleep'. We could substitute 'conscious' with 'subjective' or 'mental' or any word that arrives at the experiences we have in our minds when we sleep. Whether you've only just fallen asleep, are several hours into it, or are just about to wake up, as long as you were asleep when the conscious experience occurred, you were having a dream. It doesn't have to conform to any particular quality of dreaming. It could be as simple as having a thought about what you want to do tomorrow, or as complex as living a whole new dream-life before you wake up.[2]

WHAT IS SLEEP?

Human sleep is split into two main stages: rapid eye movement (REM) sleep, and non-REM sleep. Non-REM sleep is further divided into three more stages: Stage 1, Stage 2, and Stage 3. These different stages are characterised by various changes in the brain and body.

Stage 1 is also called 'sleep onset'. This typically lasts for about ten minutes and is the part of sleep that happens as you're first nodding off. Your eyes start to slowly roll around, and the patterns of electrical activity in your brain (i.e. your brainwaves) become bigger and slower. Starting out as medium-frequency alpha waves while you are awake but relaxed, they gradually transition to the lower-frequency theta waves.

Stage 2 comes after sleep onset. In this stage of sleep, we still have theta brainwaves, and we also have two kinds of sudden bursts of electrical activity that characterise this stage of sleep: 'sleep spindles' and 'k-complexes'. This stage is sometimes called 'light sleep'.

Stage 3, also called slow-wave sleep (SWS), or 'deep sleep', comes next. Here we transition to very big, and very slow, delta brainwaves (very low frequency). Your eyes don't move, your muscles don't move; you're deep, deep in slumber. If someone manages to drag you out of Stage 3 sleep, you'll probably be pretty grumpy with them for it.

REM sleep brainwave activity looks very similar to wakefulness – so similar, in fact, that REM used to be known as 'paradoxical sleep' because you look like you are awake (brainwave-wise) when you are actually asleep. As the present-day name suggests, REM is characterised by very quick, very large eye movements, and also muscle atonia – we are paralysed during REM sleep.

For the average person, non-REM sleep dominates the first half of the night, with REM sleep periods much more frequent and much longer in the second half of the night. A sleep cycle, which takes us through the non-REM stages and then into REM, lasts for about 90 minutes, so if you slept for seven and a half hours, you would have gone through five sleep cycles.

WHAT ARE DREAMS LIKE?

Dreams are extremely varied and are almost always a completely unique experience. However, there are some aspects of dreams that stand out as being common across many dreams.

COMMON CHARACTERISTICS

Dreams are almost always **visual**: there is almost always something you can see. You may well also hear something, feel something, taste something, or smell something, but seeing something is pretty much ubiquitous in dreams.[3]

Many dreams involve some kind of **world simulation**, or virtual reality.

Dreams are often **embodied**. We regularly have our own physical bodies in our dreams, and in these bodies, we go around in our dream-world, meeting people and doing things.

Within this embodied simulation, sometimes the dream feels like a **narrative**. It's hard to know for sure whether this is how the dream really plays out, or whether we imagine it to be this way when we're awake, but they often feel story-like.

Even within the narrative, however, dreams often **suddenly change**. We jump from one place to another, people change identity, and so on. This usually doesn't feel odd at the time.

Dreams almost always feel **real** when we experience them, even when they are bizarre and have sudden changes. We hardly ever know that we are actually in the virtual reality of our dream rather than the external reality of our waking lives. (The exception here is when we have lucid dreams: see Chapter 6.)

Dreams are a highly **social** affair. We very often spend time with other people in our dreams: sometimes people we know, sometimes people we don't know.

Emotion is often present in our dreaming world. We may feel scared, happy, angry, confused, anxious, awed, in love, guilty, or any other emotion in our dreams.

Our **fortunes** in our dreams often don't seem to be up to us. We may encounter much misfortune that wasn't our fault (e.g. accidents, illnesses, falling over, natural disasters), or we may encounter good fortune in which happier things occur.

Another common feature of dreams is **threat**. We're often faced with something or someone who wants to harm us in some way.

The way we react to this also varies: sometimes we fight; sometimes we flee.

When we awaken, dreams often seem **bizarre**. Although they do simulate our waking world in many ways, they also often contain things that are completely incongruous with what we would encounter in the waking world.

Although these are common features of dreams, some dreams may have none of them. Some dreams are simple thoughts, or plans for the next day, or static images, or geometric shapes. We look at all conscious experiences during sleep to see what's going on in our minds across the whole night of sleep, whichever stage we're in, and however long we've been asleep, which means dreams can come in all shapes and sizes, and what shape they take depends to some extent on which stage of sleep we're in.

DREAMS IN DIFFERENT SLEEP STAGES

REM SLEEP DREAMS

During REM sleep, we have our most stereotypical 'dream-like' dreams, with the common characteristics mentioned before, like world simulation, bizarre occurrences, a narrative feel, and strong emotions. They also tend to be relatively long. When you wake up and think to yourself, "That was such a crazy dream!", it's likely it was a REM dream. Dreams from REM are very common, too; you're much more likely to be dreaming during REM sleep than any of the stages of non-REM.

Dreams can be so vivid and feel so real in this stage of sleep that we actually experience them in our brains and bodies as if we were acting them out in waking reality. The muscle atonia (paralysis of the body) that we experience in REM prevents us from acting out our dreams.

This muscle paralysis can go wrong, though. People who suffer from something called 'REM sleep behaviour disorder' (RBD) stop being paralysed during REM and may act out their dreams. For example, Isabelle Arnulf, who treats RBD patients, reported that one patient dreamt "that he was a police duck flying after a pigeon thief. Meanwhile, his wife observed him squatting on the bed, waving his arms as if flying, and shouting the two-tone sound of a siren while also mimicking a duck's voice" (Arnulf, 2019).

On the flip side of this, some individuals don't lose their muscle atonia but instead continue to be paralysed after they have woken up, and this is often accompanied by terrifying nightmarish experiences, known as sleep paralysis nightmares. We'll talk about these in Chapter 6.

NON-REM DREAMS

Not all dreams are bizarre adventures, however. Some dreams are much more like waking reality. Have you ever dreamt that you were at work, and then when you woke up, you realised it was just a dream and you *actually* had to go to work? These sorts of dreams are more typical for non-REM sleep: they are more similar to our waking reality, more obviously related to concerns from our waking lives, and also shorter in duration. Sometimes non-REM dreams are less narrative than REM dreams as well, more like the kind of abstract thoughts we have in waking life.

Non-REM dreams also differ depending on which of the three stages you're in. Stage 1 dreams, for example, are often accompanied by dream imagery of falling, which you might experience as a 'jump' in your body. We call dreams from Stage 1 'hypnagogia'. We have fewer non-REM dreams than REM dreams, and Stage 3 (deep, slow-wave sleep) dreams are especially rare.

Non-REM sleep can also involve moving around during sleep, in the form of sleep-walking, sleep-eating, sleep-sex, or even sleep-texting. When performing these various sleep actions, the brain is partially awake and partially asleep. Sometimes the actions occur without accompanying dream content, and sometimes they are accompanied by dreams.

TYPES OF DREAMS

As well as looking at dreams from different sleep stages, we can also categorise dreams that have common qualities to them, such as the following types.

RECURRENT DREAMS

These are dreams which seem to occur over and over again. Some of these are shared by many people, such as losing all of your teeth at once (see also 'typical dreams' below), while others are unique to the individual. Recurrent themes can also be experienced in which the dream is very different every time, but a single theme repeats, such as a past relationship on which you never got closure. These kinds of dreams may relate to some unresolved issue(s) from waking life.

TYPICAL DREAMS

There are some dreams which many people experience, even across different cultures. These are called 'typical dreams', and researchers have documented a number of them, such as losing your teeth, being chased, arriving too late to something, flying, and being naked in public. Most people will experience some typical dreams in their lifetime but not necessarily all of them.

LUCID DREAMS

If you are aware that you are dreaming, then you are having a lucid dream. In some lucid dreams, you may also have a degree of influence over the dream and your actions within it. There's a whole section of the book dedicated to this (see Chapter 6).

NIGHTMARES

Nightmares are very unpleasant, scary dreams, which often revolve around themes of danger and threat. Some oneirologists define nightmares as only those dreams in which the emotion is so intense that it wakes you up out of your sleep. We will discuss nightmares in several different chapters: 'regular' nightmares (Chapter 3), nightmares following trauma (Chapter 4), and sleep paralysis nightmares (Chapter 6).

PRECOGNITIVE DREAMS

Across the world and throughout history, the idea that dreams can predict the future has been powerfully seductive, but is there any scientific basis to this notion? Chapter 6 delves into this.

BIG DREAMS

This type of dream was first categorised by Carl Jung. 'Big' dreams are very memorable dreams that have a big impact on the dreamer. They may include encounters with mythical creatures, instil intense emotions like awe or terror, and are often replete with archetypes (which Jung claimed were universal symbols of human existence, like 'the wise old wo/man'). Big dreams are contrasted with 'little' dreams, which are much more common and more clearly relate to aspects of waking life.

CHILDREN'S DREAMS

Some research has found that children's dreams are very different from adults' dreams and that dream content changes as we grow from infant to adult: starting as simple, often static images, and gradually developing into full-blown dreams as we enter adolescence.[4]

ANIMAL DREAMS

Do animals dream? Human animals certainly do; but what about other apes, other mammals, and other species? This question is still open for debate – we don't have a definitive answer yet.[5]

HOW DO ONEIROLOGISTS RESEARCH DREAMS?

There's a lot that can be said on this topic. Dream research is a pretty tricky thing because, unlike with sleep, we have no objective measurements of dreaming. To be able to research dreams, we have to ask people what they've been dreaming. In other words, we work with dream reports. There's a number of different ways that we collect dream reports from our volunteers, all with their own advantages and pitfalls.

COLLECTING DREAM REPORTS

Ideally, we want to collect dream reports as soon as the person wakes up so that the dream is as fresh in their memory as possible. We also want to collect lots of dreams because dreams are so varied that we need a large number of them to be able to get a general feel for them.

SLEEP LABORATORY

The 'gold standard' of collecting dream reports is in a sleep laboratory, which sounds more clinical than it is; participants get their own bedroom, which we try and make as comfy and homely as possible (although, to be fair, they do have to sleep with wires attached to their heads, which may not be all that comfy). This method ensures a high level of control and consistency. In the lab, we can measure participants' sleep with polysomnography (a graphical representation of sleep using brainwaves, eye movements, and muscle activity). Usually, participants will be repeatedly woken up throughout the night so that researchers can collect their dream reports. This method leads to high levels of dream recall as well as the dreams being recorded immediately after they occurred, therefore minimising forgetting and confabulation.

But there are downsides to the sleep lab. It is very time consuming and costly to run a sleep lab, and often we can only run an experiment with one or two participants at a time. This is problematic because we need enough people to do the experiment to be able to perform statistical analyses on the data. If we don't have enough people, the data may not be very useful. So, to obtain enough participants in a sleep lab, you need to have a lot of time and a lot of money.

Another downside to the sleep lab is that it lacks something psychologists call 'ecological validity', which means it's not very much like the real world. Having someone watch your sleep data on a computer screen while you sleep with wires stuck to your head, in an unfamiliar room, with someone waking you up repeatedly to ask you what you're dreaming, is not very similar to how people sleep naturally at home. And we know that this does affect the research because dreams collected in the lab are different to regular dreams in various ways, one of which is that people dream about the sleep lab itself about 20% of the time that they're dreaming in the lab (Schredl, 2008). This is not very helpful if we want to record the kinds of dreams they normally have.

DREAM DIARIES

A method of collecting dream reports higher in ecological validity is to ask participants to record their own dreams at home. This removes the necessity for a researcher to remain up all night with the participant, removes the expense of the sleep lab itself, and provides more naturalistic conditions under which to collect the dream reports.

This may involve giving participants portable equipment to wear (like a headband that measures brainwaves); it may involve asking them to set alarms themselves to keep waking up in the night to record their dreams; or it may involve simply asking them to keep a dream diary whenever they happen to recall a dream spontaneously. You can also collect data from many people concurrently, rather than one at a time, and it costs much less to run this kind of study. So it's both more naturalistic, and you're likely to get a much larger number of people taking part.

Another advantage of dream diaries is that they enable us to collect longitudinal data – data that's collected over a long period of time. Some dream diary research asks participants to only record dreams for a week or two, but it can also make use of the dream diaries that some individuals keep for their own reasons for months, years, even lifetimes if they are happy to provide researchers with these diaries for analysis. This method enables us to see how dreams change over the course of a person's life, and how life events affect their dreams.

The disadvantages to this method are essentially the mirror opposite of the sleep lab method: less control, more potential for memory biases, less sophisticated measurement of sleep. Another potential disadvantage to this method is the amount of time participants are asked to put into the research. They might be asked to keep a dream diary for a month, for example. For many people, this is too big a commitment, as setting aside time to write down dreams every morning may be a luxury they don't have.

QUESTIONNAIRES

This leads us to our next option for collecting dream data: questionnaires. Asking participants to fill in a simple questionnaire about their dreams is the least time-consuming option for participants, which means obtaining larger numbers of people who take part than dream diary studies or a sleep lab – numbering in the hundreds or even thousands.

The biggest drawback to questionnaires is that for many people dreams are just not very fresh in their memory, so asking people to answer questions such as "How often do you dream about your relationships?" or "How often are your dreams very scary?" might not elicit accurate answers because it's hard to remember. There's been a fair bit of research showing that our best guesses about what our dreams are like when we rely on memory alone are not very well aligned with what we actually dream about when we keep dream diaries. As such, questionnaires about dream-life, despite the advantage of being quick and easy for participants, are not usually the preferred method of collecting dream data in oneirology.

MOST RECENT DREAM

This method is exactly as it sounds: participants record the most recent dream they can recall having, however long ago it was. Like questionnaires, this method is quick and easy for participants, meaning we can collect a lot of data with this method, and it has the advantage of being about a specifically recalled dream rather than attempting to estimate one's dream-life in general. Ideally, when using this method, only participants who can recall a dream from the previous night, and no more than a week ago, would be included, since dreams older than that are likely to be misremembered. A big limitation of this method is that we get to collect only one dream per person, and given how extraordinarily varied our dreams are, it's impossible to get an understanding of a person's general dream-life with a single dream.

DREAM DATABASES

It's also possible to use existing collections of dreams to conduct research. Some of the dream diaries and 'most recent dreams' that have been collected by researchers are freely available online for researchers to use. For example, www.dreambank.net has over 20,000 dreams hosted in its collection, and www.sleepanddreamda tabase.org has over 25,000. Anyone can visit these websites and take a look at these dream collections, and researchers can utilise them to answer specific questions.

INTERVIEWS

So far, we've only talked about methods that involve collecting dream reports or filling in questionnaires. Don't we want to know what people think about their own dreams, too? Absolutely we do! For this, interviews are good. Participants keep a dream diary for a while (say a month) and then attend an interview with a researcher to talk about them. Depending on what the researcher is interested in, they may discuss any number of things about the dreams they've had. This method is good for being able to get really detailed data and involving the participants much more than when we just ask for dream reports. This is another time-consuming method, though, and another one that involves quite a bit of effort from participants, so sample sizes tend to be low-but the data tends to be very rich.

DREAM GROUPS

Another method that actively involves the participants is dream groups. In this method, participants attend a dream group, which is a session with several people discussing one person's dream, usually lasting around an hour or two. From this kind of research, we can go in-depth with the dreams and often find surprising connections with waking life from having these lengthy discussions, giving researchers really detailed data about how dreams reflect our waking lives. Participants often find that these discussions help them find things out about themselves too.

BRAIN IMAGING

Finally, an emerging method that is being used more and more these days is brain imaging. There are various different types of equipment that can be used to see what is going on in the brain while we sleep and while we dream. Some allow us to see the activity on the surface of the brain (such as electroencephalography, EEG), while others allow us to see activity much deeper in the brain (such as functional magnetic resonance imaging, fMRI). We'll explore this in more detail in the next chapter.

Once we've collected the data, we then need to analyse it. Sometimes we perform statistical tests, such as comparing the dreams of one group of people against the dreams of another (say, women's dreams versus men's dreams); other times we use more qualitative methods, such as looking for themes in a series of interviews we've conducted with people about their dreaming life.[6]

2

A BRIEF HISTORY OF DREAMS

FROM ANCIENT PHILOSOPHERS TO NEUROSCIENTISTS

Now that we've defined dreams and had a look at how oneirologists research them, I'm going to take you through a whistle-stop tour of how dreams have been treated and explored by dream enthusiasts from the dawn of time (well, the dawn of recorded history, at least) to the present day, in four stages: ancient and medieval accounts of dreaming; psychoanalysis in the early-mid 20th century; cognitive psychology from the 1950s onwards; and neuroscience in the late 20th and early 21st century.

BEFORE THE 20TH CENTURY: ANCIENT AND MEDIEVAL ACCOUNTS OF DREAMING

Dreams have been integral to human culture all over the world and throughout human history. In many ancient and medieval accounts of dreaming, dreams were often seen as prophetic, gifts from the gods, communications with ancestors, or as having some other kind of religious or spiritual meaning. In others, dreams were seen more mundanely, such as in terms of being related to our personal waking lives. This is a huge and fascinating topic, but it is not the focus of this particular book, so we will have to suffice ourselves with a brief glimpse of older accounts of dreaming to ground us in the context from whence our modern understandings and experiments with dreams came.[1]

Surviving texts from ancient Egypt and Mesopotamia (an area that now encompasses parts of Iraq, Syria, and Turkey) show us that at least as far back as the 13th century BCE – that's well over three thousand years ago – people were interested in trying to decode their dreams to find out what their future held (Hughes, 2000). In Egypt, a 'dream book' contained instructions for how to turn dreams into fortune-telling. It explains, for example, that looking at a window in a dream is a good omen and means the dreamer's cry will be heard by a god; but if a man dreams of his bed catching fire, this is a bad omen and means he is driving his wife away. This is the oldest existing form of something that we still see in bookshops all over the world today: the 'dream dictionary'.

The thinkers and writers of ancient Greece and Rome also had much to say about dreams. Aristotle was so interested in dreams that he wrote a whole treatise on them, *On Dreams*, dating back to 350 BCE. And dream incubation – visiting a temple to sleep and dream of a god or goddess to gain their favour, perhaps to be healed – was a very popular form of dream divination, centred around the healing god Asclepius. A couple of centuries later, Artemidorus wrote the *Oneirocritica*, one of the very first ancient Greek books to repeat what had been attempted in Egypt earlier: to enable people to interpret their dreams.

Going farther east, surviving ancient texts from India and Tibet also talk about dreams. The *Upanishads* is an ancient Sanskrit text which discusses the philosophy of Hinduism and is thought to have been composed in Northern India sometime between 800 and 300 BCE. In part of this text, dreaming is presented as one of four possible states of consciousness, and dreams are discussed as a philosophical exercise, with questions pondered such as "What is the difference between a dream and waking experience?", "Where does the sense of 'I' go in dreamless sleep?", and "What is continuous between the waking world and the dream world?" (Easwaran, 2007).

Other religious texts across the world have similarly pondered on the meaning of dreams and where they come from. The holy books of monotheistic religions also contain many references to dreams: for example, in the Old Testament, it is recorded that Jacob dreamt of a ladder to heaven; in the New Testament, Joseph dreams of Mary's conception of Jesus.

Fast forward about a thousand years, and the Tibetan *Bardo Thodol* describes the 'bardos' of Tibetan Buddhism: states of consciousness that exist between birth and rebirth (Baldock, 2013). One of these is the bardo of the dreamworld, which occurs every night. A spiritual practice called 'dream yoga' – techniques to enhance awareness of one's own consciousness, and of the dream state – was developed to aid clarity and self-awareness when one experiences the dream bardo (Norbu, 2002).

In the Middle Ages in Europe, interest in dreams continued. Macrobius, a Roman writer of the 5th century CE, followed in the footsteps of Aristotle as a general dream theorist. He divided dreams into those that have some sort of predictive or prophetic property and those that do not. Gregory the Great, also known as Pope Gregory I, on the other hand, was more interested in dreams from a Christian perspective; he categorised dreams based on where they came from: God, demon, or simply having a full belly (Peden, 1985).

In the later Middle Ages, interest in dreams continued the traditions of ancient Egypt and Greece in producing dream handbooks. The *Somnia Danielis* is a medieval manuscript dating to around 1400 CE, in which common dreams and their meanings were listed. The book was dedicated to the prophet Daniel from the Old Testament, though the dreams are not literally meant to be his dreams.

There are far more historical and cultural interpretations of dreams than can be explored in this brief overview, but it illustrates that the fundamental questions of "What are dreams?", "Where do dreams come from?", and "What are dreams for?" have been pondered in secular, religious, and spiritual contexts all across the world, as far back as recorded history will allow us to peer. Many of the questions and topics that are studied now in psychology have their origins in these ancient thoughts. For example, you'll find modern-day psychologists researching the relationship between dreams and waking life throughout the book but especially in this chapter, the symbolic meanings of dreams in Chapter 3, and the future-telling potential of dreams as well as the kind of self-aware dreaming first explored in India and Tibet in Chapter 6.

EARLY TO MID-20TH CENTURY: PSYCHOANALYSIS

In the early 20th century, oneirology had a huge makeover thanks to perhaps the most famous oneirologist of them all, Sigmund Freud.

FREUD'S THEORY OF DREAMS

Freud contrasted his theory with ancient interpretations of dreams. He emphasised that his theory centred dreams in the human mind, not in gods, and that they tell us about our present state of mind rather than our future fortunes.

Freud agreed with the ancients in one matter, however: that dreams are symbolic. Published in 1900, his book *The Interpretation of Dreams* led many to think his theory was all about dreams symbolising sexual desires. Freud was a bit miffed about this, but while this certainly wasn't the only thing he had to say about dreams, it's easy to understand why people thought this, as we'll see in a moment.

THE DREAM IS THE ATTEMPT TO FULFIL A WISH

Freud believed that dreams represent the attempted fulfilment of a wish from waking life. Sometimes the wish appears in the dream exactly as it exists in waking life. But if the wish is something we have repressed in the unconscious 'id' (the part of the mind Freud believed was responsible for basic urges and desires) because it's not socially acceptable, or it's embarrassing, or in some other way doesn't bear thinking about, then the dream 'censors' the wish using various kinds of distortions, including symbolism. For example, sexual or aggressive impulses may be symbolically expressed in a dream. In this way, it hides the true meaning of the dream. Freud coined the terms 'manifest content' and 'latent content' to describe the two aspects of a dream: the dream imagery itself (manifest) and the underlying wish (latent).

Freud explained several ways in which latent wishes from waking life become manifest dream imagery, such as 'condensation' (many thoughts condensed into a single dream image, such as several different people represented in one dream character), and 'displacement' (repressed emotions are attributed to apparently unrelated dream images, explaining why some dreams elicit strong emotions that seem inappropriate for the actual dream content).

This, Freud said, was one function of dreams: to release the tension created by repressing these unwelcome wishes. Another was to protect sleep; Freud called dreams 'guardians of sleep'. He believed dream distortions were necessary in order for the desire to be expressed, on the one hand, but not to wake up the dreamer on the other.

PSYCHOANALYSIS AND FREE ASSOCIATION

In order to 'translate' dream symbolism, an expert psychoanalyst was needed. The psychoanalytic method that Freud developed to 'decode' dream symbols was called *free association*. In this method, a part of the dream was first chosen, and then the analyst asked the patient questions about their associations to it. The patient then free associates: says everything they can think of that comes into their head in relation to this part of the dream, which may take them far away from the original dream imagery. In so doing, the unconscious, repressed wish behind the dream should be able to emerge.

SEXUAL SYMBOLISM

As I said earlier, Freud is well known for his thoughts on sexual symbolism, and it's not hard to see why when you read his book. He gives countless examples of dreams his patients had that he interpreted as sexual symbols. Here's just a few examples:

A woman dreams: "I arrived at the market too late, and could get nothing from either the butcher or the greengrocer woman".

Freud explains that this exact situation had arisen the day before the dream was experienced, but he wasn't satisfied with this simple explanation. For him, the obvious association to the dream was the phrase "the meat-shop was closed". (Apparently in Freud's society at the time, the phrase "the meat shop is open" was a euphemism for "your fly is undone".)

A woman dreams: "I am wearing a straw hat of peculiar shape, the middle piece of which is bent upwards, while the side pieces hang downwards".

The woman could produce no associations of her own to this oddly shaped hat, but Freud wrote that "The hat is really a male genital organ".

A woman dreams: "I arrange the centre of a table with flowers for a birthday".

This, Freud said, was a symbol for female genitalia.

What about dreams that are full of fear or anxiety, critics wanted to know. Again, Freud appealed to symbolism. Since the dream disguises the wish, it comes out in a very different way in the dream. Anxiety dreams, he said, are dreams of "sexual content . . . transformed into anxiety".

PUTTING FREUD IN A NUTSHELL

If we put Freud's dream theory in a nutshell, it boils down to some key points: dreams represent the fulfilment of unconscious, repressed wishes from waking life; the dream censor distorts the wish through symbolism and other disguises; many but not all of these unacceptable wishes are sexual in nature, so dreams are full of sexual symbolism; and an expert psychoanalyst is required to help the dreamer 'decode' the dream (find the latent content from the manifest) via the method of free association.

Now that we have understood the theory of dreams from the 'grandfather' of dream psychology, let's look at what developed soon after his theory by his one-time protégé, Carl Gustav Jung.

JUNG'S THEORY OF DREAMS

Jung was a student of Freud's dream theory, but he soon moved away from Freud and developed his own thoughts. He wrote, as early as 1934, "The view that dreams are merely the imaginary fulfilments of repressed wishes is hopelessly out of date" (Jung, 1934).

COMPENSATION

Jung believed that dreams balance waking consciousness. In the same way that bodies are self-regulating – for example, we regulate our own body temperature and glucose levels – so too, said Jung, are our minds. He said that when we have thoughts that are somehow unbalanced, we have dreams to compensate for this by representing an opposing view. If an individual had an entirely overly grandiose opinion of themselves, they might dream of themselves in a much humbler position. Conversely, if they valued themselves too little, a compensatory dream would elevate their position.

Like Freud, Jung agreed that the conscious mind may repress a thought or attitude that then emerges in a dream. Other times, compensation may happen because the waking mind has simply not considered the unconscious attitude, rather than repressed it. In one sense, Jung's theory is similar to Freud's; both men thought that dreams pictured unconscious, repressed thoughts, but while Freud thought they were all wishes (many sexual in nature), Jung's idea was broader and encompassed any thought or attitude from the mind.

OTHER KINDS OF DREAMS

As well as compensatory, Jung discussed many other kinds of dreams. Some are 'prospective' – they look to the future – and others are 'reactive' – they simply replicate very emotional experiences from one's life without any compensation and without looking forward into the future.

Jung also gave us some of the taxonomy of dreams that we still use now; for example, 'typical dreams', 'recurrent dreams', 'big' (and 'little') dreams, as we encountered in Chapter 1.

SYMBOLISM AND THE UNCONSCIOUS

Jung agreed with Freud that dreams can be symbolic, but while Freud thought dreams are symbolic in order to distort a repressed wish, Jung saw dream symbolism more simply as the *natural language* that dreams speak in. He compared dream language to story-telling, especially ancient stories like myths, parables, and similes. In ancient literature, symbolism was a very common way of expressing abstraction; even today we use metaphorical language to express abstract concepts, such as love or freedom. Dream-language is phylogenetically old, he said: it has been handed down to us from our ancestors, surviving as a means of unconscious expression.

PERSONAL AND COLLECTIVE UNCONSCIOUS

Jung described two types of the unconscious. The first is the personal unconscious, which is the part of the mind of which we are not consciously aware. This includes our suppressed/repressed memories and 'the shadow' (parts of one's personality with which the ego does not identify and therefore suppresses, such as aggressive tendencies). In dreams, the shadow could appear as a character who in some way opposes the ego of the dreamer in a compensatory way.

The second is the collective unconscious. This is the aspect of the unconscious that is shared by humans world-wide: knowledge, images, instincts, and archetypes that he claimed are inherited at birth. For Jung, archetypes are universal symbols of human existence that manifest in images that appear in dreams, as well as in art, religion, and mythology. For example, the figure of the Great Mother as an archetype of maternal love and birth.

In dreams that emerge from the personal unconscious, dream symbols are unique to that dreamer; in dreams that come from the collective unconscious, we might see symbolic figures and objects that are highly recognisable to many, like "dragons, helpful animals, and demons" (Jung, 2002).

AMPLIFICATION

Jung also developed a new method of dream analysis called *amplification*. In this kind of analysis, dream images are 'amplified' on three levels: personal, cultural, and archetypal. Associations are made between the dream imagery and the dreamer's own waking life, aspects of their shared culture, and mythical and historical meanings (such as fairy tales, fables, and myths). The archetypal amplifications tap into the collective unconscious. Unlike Freud's free association, amplification sticks closely to the dream images.

PUTTING JUNG IN A NUTSHELL

Jung's dream theory is harder to put in a nutshell as it is more complex, but main points include the following: dreams compensate for thoughts or attitudes that are repressed or under-realised in waking consciousness and help achieve psychic balance; dreams are very varied; dreams may come from the personal unconscious or from the collective unconscious; dreams are replete with symbols, archetypes, and mythology; dreams are highly symbolic in nature because they speak in the archaic language of parable and myth.

THE MODERN VERDICT ON FREUD AND JUNG

Some modern oneirologists have critiqued these theories. There are aspects about the theories that have either not stood up to scientific testing or cannot be tested scientifically. For example, later researchers who attempted to use free association concluded that this process was arbitrary, and the idea that dreams are disguised wish-fulfilments has received no experimental support.

However, there are some aspects of the theories that remain popular among oneirologists today, such as the idea that dreams can be metaphorical for waking life (as we'll see in Chapter 3) and others that have been verified through careful experimental research, such as dreaming of thoughts or memories we've suppressed.[2]

As well as this, the influence and popularity of Freud and Jung in modern psychology – both in general and in oneirology – is impossible to ignore. Although their theories were critiqued by later theorists, and other methods and theories have been developed since, there are still a great many people practicing or receiving therapy from psychoanalysts, and the ideas of Freud, Jung, and their followers continue to influence us well over 100 years after their inception. And this doesn't stop with influence in psychology: psychoanalysis has also had much influence outside of this field, such as in film, in literature, and in everyday language and thinking.

MID-TO-LATE 20TH CENTURY: THE EMERGENCE OF COGNITIVE PSYCHOLOGY

DREAMS ARE SLEEP-THOUGHTS: THE COGNITIVE THEORY OF DREAMING

While psychoanalysis dominated interest in dreams in the early 20th century, the tide began to turn in the middle of it. At this time, psychologists were beginning to think of psychology in terms of our mental processes and cognitions: things like memory, perception, and attention. This was very different from earlier ideas about human psychology, which tended to be more interested in neuroses and hidden thoughts (psychoanalysis) or in the things we actually do (behavioural psychology).

At this time, a man named Calvin Hall began to think very differently about dreams. His question was: what if dreams are simply "thinking that occurs during sleep"? (Hall, 1953). Of course, dreams are very different to the kinds of thoughts we have while awake – especially since they tend to come in the form of images and hallucinatory episodes – but, ultimately, they are a kind of cognition, a kind of thinking. Within these sleep-thoughts, we see our conceptions of ourselves and the world around us. Let's say you dreamt of yourself getting lost in a huge building; this may convey the conception you have of yourself as being lost in life. The thought that you have about it in waking life becomes an embodied experience in the dream. This instigated what he called the "cognitive theory of dreams".

Hall's second innovation was to develop a purely quantitative method of analysing dream content. Rather than a psychoanalyst giving their interpretation of a dream – which tends to result in very different interpretations depending on the analyst (i.e. is subjective) – Hall wanted a method that would give the same result every time, no matter who did the analysis (i.e. is objective). He used a method called 'content analysis', a research method that analyses the content of data – in this case, of dream reports (for example, it analyses the dream characters, the emotions felt in the dream, the locations in which the dream is set, and so forth). Hall developed a content analysis method to be used specifically for dream reports with his colleague Robert van de Castle; hence, it became known as the Hall and van de Castle (1966) method.

THE CONTINUITY HYPOTHESIS OF DREAMING

In later work, Hall developed what has become known as the 'Continuity Hypothesis' of dreaming. Hall thought Freud and Jung focused too much on 'discontinuities' between waking life and dreams, the things that were different between them, such as the latent content or compensatory aspects, which psychoanalysts believed were disguised or portrayed in symbolic form. The Continuity Hypothesis, conversely, states that aspects of waking life, like our thoughts, our behaviours, and our emotions, carry over (or continue into) dreams in very transparent, obvious ways.

CONTINUITY OF CONCEPTIONS AND CONCERNS

Hall analysed the dreams of some famous individuals, including Freud's and Jung's, as well as many others. He was able to accurately glean many details about individuals from their dreams, even with-out knowing anything else about them, such as their interests, their worries, and their relationships, and find differences between indi-viduals, such as how dreams differ between men and women.[3] For example, it was found that on average men dream more often of other men, whereas women dream of men and women roughly equally; that women dream more often of family and friends, and have more familiar and indoor settings than men; and that men dream more often of sex and aggression, and both success and failure, than women. Similar results were found during different decades and in different countries.

This method also allows us to look at a long dream series of an individual and, without knowing a single other thing about them, make accurate inferences about their lives based on what they dream about. We can make good guesses about the most important people in their lives and how their relationships with those people are; we can see when big life events occur, what things preoccupy them for long periods of time, and so on. How? Because we dream repeatedly of the things that are most important to us and are of the most concern to us, so just by looking at the content of the dream we can see what has been preoccupying someone.

Domhoff (2003), for example, used the Hall and van de Castle method to analyse a huge number of dreams of a single individ-ual, 'Barb Sanders', and then interviewed Sanders and some of her friends to see if he had gleaned accurate information about her from her dream series. And for the most part, he did. For exam-ple, her mother was the most common character in her dreams, suggesting she plays a significant role in Sanders's life; interviews confirmed that her mother was a very important (and problematic) figure in her waking life. In general, this huge body of work carried out by Hall, Domhoff, and their colleagues showed us how dreams often play out – in what feel like real experiences – the things we are thinking about, worrying about, and doing. It showed that when we dream of the same thing over and over again, that is something that is of particular concern.

CONTINUITY OF EXPERIENCES

In more recent years, researchers have been expanding on the Continuity Hypothesis and investigating which experiences from our waking lives appear in our dreams and which don't. For example, our highly emotional waking-life experiences appear in dreams more than experiences that were not very emotional (Malinowski & Horton, 2014b). And media we have been consuming often turns up in our dreams, like a film we've just watched, or a video game in which we've been immersed.

Conversely, some things on which we spend huge amounts of time during waking hours, like working on a computer if we have an office job, hardly ever appear in our dreams at all. It seems we tend not to dream much of the everyday things that we do. Even when we do dream of our experiences, we hardly ever dream about them exactly as they happened. Dreams are not just passively reflecting the things we've been doing during the day but seem to select certain things from our waking lives, like significant, emotional experiences we've had, and these are the experiences that then appear.

These sorts of findings have led some oneirologists to wonder: why is it that some aspects of waking life appear often in dreams, and others hardly ever do? This question has led to the idea that maybe there is some kind of purpose to this: that these parts of waking life are being deliberately selected over others to appear in our dreams for a reason. In Chapter 3, we will consider several different theories of dream function.

DREAMS CONTINUE INTO WAKING LIFE TOO

Continuity between waking life and dreams isn't just a one-way street. While it's clear that our waking lives influence our dreams, we also know that dreams affect our waking selves. Have you ever had a dream in which your partner was unfaithful, or you had a raging argument with a friend, or one of your loved ones passed away? Think about how you felt afterwards. It's likely that the emotions the dream brought up – anxiety, anger, sadness, and so on – spilled over into your morning, perhaps your whole day, maybe even longer. I've had many people tell me that when they dreamt of their partner cheating on them, they were mad at them for ages afterwards – sometimes even wanting an apology from them for dream-cheating.

DREAMS ARE BOTH THOUGHTS AND BRAIN ACTIVITY: THE NEUROCOGNITIVE THEORY OF DREAMS

From the turn of the 21st century onwards, the cognitive theory became the neurocognitive theory (Domhoff, 2001). This theory emphasised that not only are dreams a form of cognition which embody our concerns from waking life, but that they are only able to form in minds that are mature enough (i.e. the brain has developed enough in childhood to be able to produce dreams), in the absence of brain damage that may affect dreaming (see next section), in the absence of stimuli (i.e. the mind is not engaged with anything else at the time), and with the correct activation of certain brain regions. Dreaming, in this formulation, draws on our memories, our understandings of ourselves and our world, and our imaginations, to create simulations of our reality that depict things we are thinking about and doing in waking life. This theory is the first we have considered so far to place dreams firmly in the physical stuff of the brain (as opposed to the abstract, formless 'mind'), and it's to this that we turn in the next section.

INTO THE 21ST CENTURY: NEUROSCIENCE

Neuroscientific oneirology aims to discover what is going on behind the scenes, in our brains, when we dream. When rapid eye movement (REM) sleep was discovered in 1953, there followed a flurry of excitement amongst sleep and dream researchers. For some time, it was thought that REM sleep and dreaming were two sides of the same coin: that whenever we are in REM sleep, we are dreaming; and whenever we are dreaming, we are in REM sleep. But, of course, our brains weren't going to make it that easy for us. We now know it's far more complicated than this.

THE ACTIVATION-SYNTHESIS HYPOTHESIS

One of the most influential (and controversial) neuroscientific theories is the activation-synthesis hypothesis (Hobson & McCarley, 1977). This hypothesis placed itself in direct opposition to traditional psychoanalytical theories of dreaming. It claimed that dreams are not a result of disguised wishes, but rather are the result of the **activation** of disparate regions of the brain and the **synthesis** of the various images and memories that arise due to the activation of these parts of the brain into a dream-narrative – hence the name.

They claimed that the brainstem, a part of the brain known to be crucial to generate REM sleep, also generated dreams through a rhythmic pattern of activity called PGO waves.[4] The hypothesis goes that the brainstem, located at the back and bottom of the brain (near the top of the spine), sends random waves of activity upwards towards the forebrain. The forebrain then tries its best to make some sense of all this random activity and weaves an often-peculiar dream narrative.

The theory made some enemies because many believed that it claimed dreaming is meaningless – that it is just the synthesis of semi-random brain activity. The concept that dreams are meaningless is a myth that unfortunately still persists even now, perhaps because it is so counterintuitive and such a controversial suggestion, and everyone loves a bit of controversy. But the reality is that not even the original authors really claimed that dreams are meaningless: they were careful to state that the theory "does not deny meaning to dreams"; it only denies the classic psychoanalytical interpretation of dream meaning.

REM AND DREAMING ARE NOT THE SAME THING

The activation-synthesis model relied on the assumption that we can explain dreams by understanding the physiology of REM sleep. But the notion that REM sleep and dreaming are two sides of the same coin has been repeatedly refuted by experiments that find you can have REM sleep without dreaming, and you can dream outside of REM sleep.

This idea was solidified in the year 2000 by neuropsychologist Mark Solms, who worked with brain-damaged patients and discovered two crucial nails in the coffin for the REM = dreaming hypothesis: 1) damage to the brainstem, which results in a near or complete loss of REM sleep, does not lead to a loss of dreaming; and 2) damage to areas in the forebrain *does* lead to loss of dreaming but not to REM sleep. For most of the patients who had lost their ability to dream, damage was done not to the brainstem but to the PTO junction, an area in the brain where the parietal, temporal, and occipital lobes of the cerebral cortex meet, suggesting this area in particular may be crucial for dream generation.

THE AIM MODEL

Growing evidence that REM sleep is not the same as dreaming led to various revisions of the activation-synthesis model, until the new "AIM" model emerged. The three components of the AIM model correspond to: how Active the brain is; what Input the brain is receiving (i.e. is it awake, or is it asleep?); and how it is Modulated in terms of the neurochemicals that are in play. The model suggests that over the course of any one day these three components vary, and the ways in which they vary determine whether one is asleep or awake and dreaming or not dreaming.

For example: when we're awake, the brain is very active, it receives inputs from the outside world, and it is modulated by noradrenaline (NA) and serotonin (5-HT). When we're in REM sleep, conversely, the brain is still very active, but it is almost entirely blocked off from inputs from the outside world, and it is modulated by acetylcholine (ACh). And non-REM sleep is different to both: it is blocked off to the external world, but less active than both wakefulness and REM, and modulated by NA, 5-HT, and ACh (but has lower levels of each than either waking or REM).

WHAT YOUR BRAIN IS DOING WHEN IT DREAMS

But if we *really* want to know what's happening in the brain during dreaming, we need to look at the brain *during* dreaming. Recently, a team of researchers led by Francesca Siclari and her colleagues at the University of Wisconsin-Madison in the USA conducted a pioneering study that tried to understand what the brain is doing while it is having a dream. To do this, their participants slept in a laboratory and the researchers periodically woke them up by an alarm. When they were woken up, the participants reported on whether they were dreaming or not dreaming. If they did remember having a dream, they reported the last part of the dream that they were having just before they woke up, if they could. At the same time, their brain activity was being monitored with EEG – electrodes stuck all over the scalp.

The team found that people who *were* dreaming had a very clear neural signature: changes in activity in certain areas of the brain, especially the parietal and occipital lobes of the cortex (which sit at the top-back and back of the brain respectively), named by the authors as the "posterior hot zone".

They then used this information to try and predict whether a person is dreaming or not dreaming. The participants went to sleep again, and when the EEG readings indicated the correct combination of neural activity in the posterior hot zone, they predicted that they would be having a dream, so they woke them up and asked them. Their accuracy was impressive: 92% of the time they predicted correctly.

This is very interesting in light of Mark Solms's brain damage findings that we saw earlier. Remember how the individuals with brain damage who reported a loss of dreaming had damage to the PTO junction? This area has similarities with the 'posterior hot zone' (although the PTO junction is deeper in the brain). This area, then, when damaged, leads to a loss of dreaming, and when active, very accurately predicts dreaming. So far, then, this parietal-temporal-occipital area seems like a good contender for a neural correlate of dream generation.

They also found that areas of the brain known to be active during certain types of waking cognition were active for the same cognition during sleep. For example, when we look at a person's face when we're awake, a region called the 'fusiform face area' becomes active. Likewise, Siclari's team found that when we dream of a face, a brain region very closely related to this area is active. This shows that looking at a face in waking life, and dreaming of a face, rely on very closely related areas of the brain.

CONCLUSIONS

The neuroscience of dreaming is one of the youngest academic fields of oneirology and is reliant on expensive technology, which necessarily means that progress is slow, laborious, and relies on small sample sizes. Nevertheless, huge strides have been made, technology continues to advance, and testable theories are beginning to emerge. We know now that REM sleep and dreaming are undoubtedly not one and the same thing and that we need more than the firings of the brainstem to generate a dream. Research from brain-damaged individuals, and from a recent EEG study, shows that we need forebrain activity, perhaps especially in parietal and occipital areas of the brain, to generate a dream. Future research will shed more light on these initial tantalising findings.

Neuroscientific research has also found that when we dream, parts of our brain known to be involved in interacting with our waking world are activated. This is crucially important work because it shows that we experience dream-worlds as real and interact with them in the same way we do our waking world. Most of us already know this to be true – sometimes dreams feel even more real than waking life! But this kind of evidence is important because it shows that the feeling we have of dreams being 'real' makes sense, since our brains are indeed experiencing them as if they were real.

POSTSCRIPT TO THE BRIEF HISTORY OF DREAM RESEARCH

This book mainly shines a light on dream psychology through the lens of modern experimental psychology, which, as things stand at the time of writing, is the dominant approach to studying dreams in psychology at 'Western' universities. Readers should be aware, however, that this is only one way of conducting research. Just as religious and spiritual interpretations of dreams have been (and indeed are now for many) the preferred perspective for understanding dreaming, which faded out to a large extent in Western psychology thanks to the advent of psychoanalysis, and just as the dominant perspective of psychoanalysis gave way, to some extent, to cognitive-experimental psychology and neuroscience in the mid and late portions of the 20th century and the early 21st century, so today's perspectives will inevitably be replaced in the future with something new again.

In this sense, this book is itself a snapshot historical text – today it is cutting edge; next century it may be archaic. Readers should keep this in mind as they go; read the ideas within critically, wondering what might be found if we asked different questions or used different methods or had different aims. We'll look to some possible future scenarios for dream research in Chapter 7, but what the future really holds is up to future oneirologists – perhaps some of the people reading this book. What do you want to find out next? What is experimental psychology fundamentally missing or failing to grasp? These are the sort of questions that will propel us into a new era of oneirology when the current one ebbs out of favour to be replaced by the next big ideas.

3

WHY DO WE DREAM?

MEMORY, EMOTION, CREATIVITY, AND SIMULATION THEORIES OF DREAMING

Sleep is functional. Fact. In fact, sleep is multifunctional: it does many different things for us. Sleep is crucial for memory, concentration, physical health, mental health; to be honest, it's good for just about everything.

If sleep is functional, it would make sense that dreaming is also functional, if we view dreaming as the subjective mental activity that occurs during sleep. But it may not be this simple. Sleep and dreaming are not one and the same. We are not always dreaming when we're asleep. Some stages of sleep are much more prone to dreaming than others, and dream content differs depending on which stage of sleep we're in and how long we've been asleep. For these reasons, to try and understand why we dream, we cannot only ask why we sleep and assume dreaming serves the same purpose; we need to look at the dreams themselves.

Dreaming is a complex, extremely diverse phenomenon. As such, it is highly unlikely that there will ever be a simple, single answer to the question of "why do we dream?" any more than there would be a simple answer to the questions "why do we think?" and "why are we conscious?" In this chapter, we will consider some of the most popular and well-researched theories of dreaming whilst acknowledging that this is unlikely to be the full story. Because this is a psychology book, dream function will be approached from the perspective that dreams may be *psychologically* useful to us in some way: specifically, we'll be looking at dreaming for memory, emotion, creativity, and for preparing for the future.

WAIT . . . WHAT IF DREAMS HAVE *NO* FUNCTION?

An argument that has been made fairly widely in oneirology is that dreaming may well have *no* function at all, that dreaming is a mere by-product of sleep, like the froth on a pint of beer.[1] However, plenty of functional theories exist, and it's to these that we now turn.

MEMORY CONSOLIDATION THEORIES OF DREAMING

DREAMING OF THE PAST

If you think back to any dream you had within the last week or so, there's a good chance that some part of it will feature something from your waking life. Freud called the spill-over from the day's events into dreams 'day residue', and research has provided us with plenty of evidence for it, showing that around half of our dreams contain some reference to something that happened earlier that day. We do also dream of things from further back in time, and the remoteness of the memory tends to be dependent on how long we've been asleep: in the first few hours of the night, when we're mostly having non-REM sleep, we dream of more recent experiences; then later at night, when we have much more REM sleep, we dream of our more remote memories, like ones from our childhood.[2]

It's clear that our memories form a huge part of many of our dreams: memories of people we know, places we've been, things we've seen or done, and stuff we're thinking about. When it comes to function, the fact that our dreams are full of memories has made some people wonder: is it possible that this reactivation of memories is actually helping us to remember them? Could the strengthening of our memories – or 'memory consolidation' – be a function of dreaming?

DREAMING TO REMEMBER

There's no doubt that memory consolidation (the process by which new memories become long-term memories) is a function of sleep. We need sleep *before* we make new memories, to get our brains in a state of readiness to receive this information; and we also need sleep *after* those new memories have been made, to help them become strengthened, solidified, and possible to be recalled at a later date. Sleep research is unequivocal on this. There's even a theory that lack of sleep may be instrumental in bringing about the memory deficits seen in older-age diseases like dementia and Alzheimer's. It's thought that, during sleep – especially non-REM sleep – our memories are reactivated, or replayed, and this strengthens them for future recall.

In research with non-human animals such as rats, it is possible to quite literally see the moment that a new memory is replayed and strengthened during sleep. In this kind of research, rats' brains are implanted with electrodes so that their neuronal activity can be recorded, and then they're trained to navigate their way through a little rat maze to find a treat. Groups of 'place cells' (a type of neuron in the hippocampus, a structure very important for memory) fire together when the rat is in a certain place in their environment, creating a new memory of that location. Then, when the rats are asleep later, those same groupings of place cells fire together again. If the rats could tell us what they were dreaming of just then, if rats *can* dream,[3] it would be a good guess that they were dreaming of being back in that location in the maze.

In human research, we rely on dream reports, since different ethical rules apply to humans compared to rats and other non-human animals (e.g. implanting electrodes in healthy human brains is not permitted). As we saw in Chapter 1, dream reports taken from REM sleep differ from dream reports taken from non-REM sleep. This is important for the memory consolidation theory of dreams because it maps rather neatly onto what we know about how different types of memories are consolidated by different stages of sleep. For example, episodic memories – memories for events from our waking lives – need a healthy dose of non-REM sleep for consolidation. But emotional memories – those with high levels of emotions, like fear – are better served by REM sleep. If dreams really do reflect these sleep processes, then we should see dreams that match up to the types of memories consolidated in these different sleep stages.

And this is exactly what we do see. In non-REM sleep, we are much more likely to have dreams that clearly depict an event from our waking lives than in REM sleep. Likewise, in REM sleep, we are much more likely to have very emotionally charged dreams than we are in non-REM sleep. So this is all well and good so far: we definitely dream about our memories, and we dream about the right memories in the right stages of sleep to map onto their memory consolidation during sleep, so this might be evidence that dreams are the conscious experience of that consolidation process.

However, the fact that we dream of our memories doesn't necessarily mean dreams are an *active* part of this process. It could be that dreams merely *reflect* the sleep process rather than contribute to it. What we really need now for this theory to hold up is evidence that dreams actually actively contribute to the strengthening of memories rather than just reflect memories.

In 2010, sleep researcher Erin Wamsley had her participants playing a skiing game called *Alpine Racer*, an arcade game in which the player stands on a pair of skis and negotiates virtual snow-encrusted slopes. She found that many people dreamt of the game and that those who were worst at it at the beginning dreamt of it the most. This made these researchers wonder: did dreaming so much about the game actually make them better at it?

This question was answered by her next experiment. This time her participants had to run around in a virtual reality maze. After that, half of them went for a nap, and half of them stayed awake. Wamsley collected dream reports from the sleeping participants, and daydream reports from the awake participants. When they went back into the virtual maze later, they were scored on how quickly they could navigate it. Her results were amazing: not only did the participants who slept do better than those who hadn't slept, but the participants who had slept *and dreamt of the maze* did better than those who slept and *didn't* dream of the maze. But there was no advantage to having daydreams of the maze. This seemed to show quite neatly that it's not just sleep but sleep *plus dreaming of the memory* that's needed for consolidation, whereas daydreaming doesn't work the same way.[4]

On the other hand, the people who did dream of the maze weren't replaying themselves running around in the maze, the way we had imagined the rats doing. For example, two of the maze dreams included only the *music* from the maze, and another one was a memory of a "maze-like" bat cave the participant had visited in the past. So the dreams only *vaguely* related to the maze rather than replaying the maze experience directly, which means that if the dreams are contributing to consolidation, they're doing so without them reactivating the memories exactly as they happened but by calling up dreams that are somewhat related to the maze.

In fact, this kind of thing has happened in many different studies. In one, in which participants were given 'inversion goggles' to wear while they were awake (which made them see the world upside-down), those who dreamt of things related to being upside down were better able to cope with their newly inverted world when they woke up (de Koninck et al., 1996). But again, they didn't actually *rehearse* being upside down in their dreams. Instead, they dreamt of things like this: "I looked at a word but it was upside-down". The dreams were related to inversion but weren't of actually *being* inverted. The same has been noted in people learning a new language: dreaming of the language was associated with improvements on it, but no one was clearly practicing the language in their dreams (de Koninck et al., 1988, 1990).

This relates to dreaming of our general waking-life memories too, because although we do dream of things from our lives often, we very rarely dream about a whole, intact memory. A study I conducted a few years ago found that in almost 200 dreams I recorded from participants, only one of them was very clearly a memory of an entire event from that person's life (Malinowski & Horton, 2014a). The rest of the time, the memories were fragmented and appeared in isolation, in totally new dream scenes, and often alongside other unrelated memories. For example, someone might have dreamt of being in the world of *The Walking Dead*, fighting off zombies (one memory) with their best friend (another memory) and in a place that reminded them of somewhere they'd been on holiday as a child (a third memory). Clearly, they have not experienced this actual dream event; rather, the dream is populated by different aspects of several memories and creates something entirely new.

WHY ARE MEMORIES IN DREAMS JUMBLED UP?

Because of all of this, it has become clear that memories are not simply reactivated and replayed in dreams in the exact same way they originally happened. Instead what happens is that pieces, or fragments, of memories are activated in combination with other seemingly unrelated memory fragments all together. This combination always leads to a new, unique dream. This makes sense if we bear in mind that human memory is actually really not about remembering things exactly as they happened – we rarely manage this, in fact. The way memory really works is that new memories are slotted into ones we already have, and we try to make sense of new experiences by comparing them with ones we've already had. It follows logically, then, that these memories are played in conjunction with other ones: sometimes other new ones and sometimes old ones we've had for a long time. This has the effect of avoiding 'overwriting' old memories with new ones and instead *integrating* new memories with older ones.

SO DO WE DREAM TO REMEMBER, OR NOT?

We know for sure that sleep helps us to remember and that we dream of memories, both new and old ones. We also know that when we dream of something new that we need to remember, we actually do remember it better. But we also know that the dreams we have of those new memories are strange – we don't rerun the maze or rehearse the new language. Rather, we have dreams that are *associated* somehow to those new memories – we might dream of a maze-like cave or of being annoyed that we can't speak the new language. Why exactly it happens this way, and how this contributes to memory consolidation, is still something of a mystery but may have to do with the need to decontextualise new memories and slot them in with the ones we already have rather than remember them exactly as they happened.

EMOTION-PROCESSING THEORIES OF DREAMING

The idea that dreams help us to work through our emotions might be the most well-known functional theory of dreams; certainly, it is one of the most written about. Several oneirologists have written whole books on this idea, notably Ernest Hartmann and Rosalind Cartwright; details of their books dedicated to this topic are given at the end of this book. The general idea is that when we dream of our previous experiences, especially ones that are emotional, this is one of the brain's ways of processing and making sense of those experiences and ultimately making them feel less emotional.

THE NOCTURNAL THERAPIST

Just as sleep research has shown unequivocally that sleep is crucial for memory, so it has shown that it is also crucial for mood and emotion regulation. When we're sleep deprived, we 'overreact' emotionally, both to positive and negative experiences, in comparison to when we've had a good night's sleep. Sleep disturbance is a symptom of pretty much every mood disorder that has been catalogued, including depression and anxiety disorders. Sleep is so important for us to be able to regulate our mood and our emotional reactions that some researchers have called it "overnight therapy" (Walker & van der Helm, 2009). Every night as we sleep, we consolidate, process, integrate, and try to make sense of the emotional experiences we've had in waking life and get ourselves ready to be able to face and process new ones the next day.

And, as is the case with memory, dreams reflect this nocturnal activity. They are often full of things we are concerned about in our waking lives. If you've got an exam coming up that you're worried about, you may dream about failing it. If you're worried about the security of your relationship, you might dream of your partner cheating on you. Dreams so reliably and consistently portray our anxieties and fears that when researchers look at an individual's dream series, without knowing a single other thing about that person, they can tell things like which members of their family they are most worried about, what their relationship with their partner is like, when they have a new love interest, and so forth. Likewise, we all dream of all manner of other life-changing events: deaths of loved ones, worries about health, changing jobs, passing exams, breakups, pregnancy, and so on.

Oneirologist Rosalind Cartwright broke much ground in this topic during her work with individuals going through divorce (Cartwright, 2011). In a series of studies, volunteers who were in the process of divorcing their spouse came to her sleep lab and spent some nights sleeping there and reporting their dreams, as well as indicating how they were coping with the divorce proceedings. Some of the divorcees coped well; others didn't and ended up developing depression. Interestingly, the dreams of the divorcees who didn't get depression were different from those who did. The former had dreams that were longer, had a wider range of time frames (i.e. referring to the dreamer's past, present, and future), were more complex, and more often dealt with the dreamer's issues relating to the divorce. The depressed divorcees, conversely, dreamt less often of their marital issues, even though they were thinking about them often in waking life, and their dreams were generally either 'flatter' (less emotional) or more unpleasant. Could this be showing that their dreams actually helped the non-depressed divorcees to work through their divorce?

Cartwright made some other fascinating discoveries too. If people who weren't depressed went to bed in a bad mood, she found, their dreams started out full of negative emotions but became progressively more positive across the night, just as if the dreams were regulating the person's mood and getting them ready to start fresh in the morning. But the pattern was very different for depressed people. Their dreams started out negative *and stayed negative all night*. Actually, it was even worse than that – they started out negative and then got more negative! She also found that depressed individuals dreamt of themselves in negative ways and of having unpleasant things happening to them, especially towards the end of the night. So, instead of regulating and processing unpleasant emotions, dreams for the depressed people seemed to just make things worse. Certain types of dreams are associated with coping well with difficult life events, therefore, while other types of dreams are associated with lack of coping and depression.

However, while Cartwright's work seems promising as evidence for emotion-processing in dreams, we must consider that we cannot actually perform 'true' experiments with dreams as we can with sleep. In a sleep experiment, we can assign our volunteers to different conditions – Group A will go to sleep, and Group B will stay awake – and then see how sleeping versus not-sleeping affects people later on. We can't do this with dreams: we don't yet have reliable methods to say to one group, "You go to sleep and have a dream", and to the other "You go to sleep and don't have a dream". Therefore, the research Cartwright and others have done on emotion-processing in dreams is *correlational*: people with certain types of dreams are depressed, and people with other types of dreams are not. We can't be sure that it's the dreams that make the difference in whether or not the person is depressed, only that there is a relationship between dream content and depression.

CALMING THE STORM

The other oneirologist I mentioned at the beginning of this section, Ernest Hartmann, also had much to say about emotion-processing in dreaming. Hartmann worked with trauma survivors who had repetitive nightmares about their trauma. Nightmares, he said, picture our fears in many different ways: being chased, being engulfed by a tidal wave, being in an out-of-control car; dreams like these translate our abstract emotions into concrete, embodied, and lived (and often frightening) dream experiences.

Hartmann said that the reason for this is that dreams 'calm the storm' of waking life; they picture waking-life emotions and connect these emotions with other related experiences in order to reduce their impact and the distress they cause. Just as we saw in the memory consolidation theory, the idea is that new experiences need to be compared with and integrated with older ones in order for them to be made sense of, and, in the case of very difficult emotional experiences, coped with.

The process of dreams picturing emotional waking-life experiences and calming them is something that happens long term, especially if the experience was extremely emotional. The process has to occur repeatedly for adaptation to occur − it's not just across one night, but many nights until the experience is dealt with. For some experiences that are low in emotional intensity, this might happen very quickly. For experiences with high emotional intensity like trauma, however, it could take years. In Hartmann's work with trauma survivors, he noticed that as the trauma was gradually worked through, the dreams would change: from literal re-enactments of the traumatic experience, gradually to more 'dream-like' renditions of the experience (see Chapter 4).

DREAMS REDUCE EMOTION INTENSITY

But to really be able to argue that dreaming of an emotional experience helps us to turn down our emotions about that experience, we need evidence of this happening. In a study I conducted recently, we found exactly this.

I had become interested in something called the 'dream rebound effect'. When we try to suppress something that causes us distress to think about, we often end up dreaming of it. In other words, it 'rebounds' in our dreams. I wanted to know: when we dream about this unpleasant thought, does that make us feel better or worse about it? If dreams are helping us to process emotions, then dreaming of it should make us feel better about it.

To find this out, my participants were asked to suppress a thought every night before bed for a week, and they recorded their dreams in the mornings. They also rated how they felt about this thought at the very beginning of the study and then again at the end. I then divided participants into two groups: people who dreamt often about their suppressed thought, and participants who dreamt only rarely of it. When I compared these two groups, I found that participants who dreamt often about their suppressed thought generally felt much better about it at the end of the study. In other words, dreaming of the unpleasant thought did make them feel better: so this supports the emotion-processing theory.

Other research has found similar results. In a study in 2020 led by Virginie Sterpenich at the University of Geneva, Switzerland, volunteers slept in a sleep lab, and their brain activity was recorded at the same time. During the night, they were woken repeatedly and asked to describe what they were dreaming. During the day, they were shown faces of people, some of which were 'aversive' (i.e. were unpleasant to look at in some way), and to see how much the volunteers responded to these sorts of faces, they measured the size of their pupils. The volunteers who dreamt frequently of fear were less responsive to the aversive faces, suggesting that dreaming of fearful things has an emotion-regulation function during the day.

NIGHTMARES AND BAD DREAMS

These are dreams that are full of unpleasant emotions like fear, anxiety, or sadness. Nightmares tend to be more fear-based and revolve around threats and danger. One definition of nightmares classifies them as bad dreams that are so bad, they actually wake you up.

We all have these dreams sometimes, and while they may be horrible to experience, they may actually be helping us deal with emotions in waking life, as we saw in Virginie Sterpenich's study. Other onei-rologists have similar ideas, suggesting that we have nightmares and/

or bad dreams repeatedly about similar waking-life issues until we have come to terms with them. The nightmares may also be a kind of 'safety valve' – they allow us to express and release our negative emotions, helping us to become better at coping with them. Nightmares can also act as a kind of beacon, showing us that there's something we need to work on, which can then be explored through, for example, psychotherapy.

Conversely, some nightmares aren't helpful at all, particularly those that follow traumatic experiences and repeatedly re-expose the sufferer to their trauma while they sleep. In the case of these kinds of nightmares, treatment is likely to be needed. We consider these kinds of nightmares in the next chapter. Nightmares are also known to be related more generally to poor mental health, suggesting that if it is the case that nightmares can be helpful for some people, maybe they aren't for everyone. Differences between individuals (like whether or not they're experiencing poor mental health) and also situational factors (like what's going on in their lives at the time) affect how we experience dreams and nightmares. For some people, nightmares may be helpful; for others, they may be harmful.

IT'S NOT ALL BAD

So far, we've only really considered emotion-processing in terms of unpleasant experiences, like divorce. But we dream of wonderful things too. In fact, on the whole, we have just as many pleasant emotions in our dreams as we do unpleasant ones, and we dream just as often of our positive experiences from waking life as our negative ones. What seems to matter most is intensity: any waking-life experience you have that is accompanied by intense emotions is the sort of thing you are most likely to dream about. But if emotion-processing is a function of dreaming, why do we dream so much about things that we don't need to 'cope' with but are wonderful to experience?

I pondered these things with one of my colleagues, Caroline Horton, in a paper we wrote together for the journal *Frontiers in Psychology*

(Malinowski & Horton, 2015). We suggested that the reason we dream of our pleasant experiences as well as our unpleasant ones is because dreams aren't only helping us to cope with our harrowing or difficult experiences; they're also helping us to remember and make sense of our wonderful ones. When we have a strong emotional response to something, that's the brain's way of waving its arms, pointing to the experience, and saying, "This one! This one is important!". We need to remember the stuff that's most important; emotions automatically tell us what's most important. We need to remember which experiences were horrible and which were brilliant, so we can remember how to avoid the former and seek out the latter again in the future. So we're dreaming of both ugly *and* beautiful memories, perhaps so that we can *remember* them. In this way, memory consolidation and emotion-processing go hand-in-hand.

As well as this, dreams do need to help us down-regulate positive experiences too. It would be spectacularly unhelpful for us if, every time we recall a memory of something from our past, we react with the same emotional intensity as we did at the time. Every time we recalled a failed relationship, we'd be struck down with the same heartbreak we felt then; but equally, every time we recalled the moment we first heard "I love you", we'd be incapacitated with joy. We need to be able to 'turn down' our emotional responses to *all* of our memories, not just the negative ones, so that we're not constantly in a state of hyper-emotionality each time we remember something from our past.

This has recently been neatly demonstrated in a study by a group of researchers led by Raphael Vallat in the Lyon Neuroscience Research Centre in France. They found that when we dream of something that happened to us in waking life, the experience in the dream is much less emotional than the original waking-life experience: positive experiences from waking life became less positive in dreams, and negative experiences from waking life became less negative in dreams, while neutral experiences stayed the same. Just as we would expect according to the emotion-processing theory, emotional experiences were 'turned down' in dreams.

PROBLEM-SOLVING AND CREATIVITY THEORIES

Have you heard the phrase "sleep on it"? Say there's a problem you can't quite figure out how to solve, or something you can't quite make your mind up about. Maybe someone said to you "just sleep on it", and you did, and the next day the answer seemed much clearer. Did you ever wonder just *why* sleeping on a problem helps you to solve it? What exactly is it about the sleeping brain that suddenly gives us that eureka! moment upon awakening, or gives us the insight we need about something that seemed so intractable only yesterday? Could it be our dreams that are doing this?

INSIGHT AFTER SLEEP

Sleep scientists have conducted several experiments showing us clearly how important sleep is for insight. After sleep (compared to staying awake), we get better at all sorts of creative puzzles. In particular, REM sleep is good for this. If we extrapolate from laboratory-based experiments to real life, we can imagine that REM sleep enables us to be creative with any problem we're working on, to come up with insightful connections that we might not be able to make with the waking mind alone.

DISCOVERIES IN DREAMS

We can see just how creative dreams can be when we look at all the discoveries that have been made within them. Music, art, science, and technology have all benefited from the nightlife of various creative brains.

In music, many tales exist in which musicians have heard new music in a dream that they have then created in waking life. The Beatles' 'Yesterday', Stravinsky's *Rite of Spring*, Wagner's *Tristan and Isolde*, Queen's 'The Prophet's Song' – all of these and many other musical works are said to have come to the artists through dreams.

Similarly, there are many tales of scientific discoveries in dreams. One of the most famous examples is the chemist August Kekulé, who had been trying to figure out what the chemical structure of benzene was. One day, he is said to have had a dream in which he saw an *ouroboros* – an alchemical symbol of a snake eating its own tail – forming a circle. Upon awakening, Kekulé had an *aha!* moment and realised that this was the structure he'd been looking for: the chemical structure of benzene was a circle. Other examples include Mendeleev's invention of the periodic table and Elias Howe's invention of the sewing machine, both the result of dreams.

Entire novels have also been created within an author's dreamworld. Two of the most famous examples of these are Mary Shelley's *Frankenstein* and Robert Louis Stevenson's *The Strange Case of Dr. Jekyll and Mr. Hyde*. Both of these famous authors dreamt of their main characters before writing them into their novels.

Coming from a personal perspective, dreams have been a huge source of creative inspiration for me too. I once wrote an entire novel based on one dream I had that affected me so much I had to write it into waking life. I also sometimes come up with new ideas for work in dreams: on more than one occasion I have come up with an idea of how to teach a subject I've never taught before in a dream, and the idea was good enough that I ended up using it in the actual class.

DREAMING TO SOLVE PROBLEMS

So far, it's clear that dreams may give us flashes of creative insights. Sometimes they present something to us that we then create: a song, or a story, for example. At other times, they help us find insights into a seemingly intractable problem. Thinking about dreams as potential problem-solvers has led some researchers to wonder: what kind of dreams do people have when they actually try to solve a problem with them?

In a 1993 study led by Harvard-based oneirologist Deidre Barrett, participants actively tried to have dreams to solve a problem from their waking lives. After a week, about half of the participants had had a dream about the problem, and the majority of these had a dream that helped solve the problem. For example, one student had applied to a few different university programmes and couldn't decide which one to go for. She dreamt that she was in a plane over Massachusetts, and the pilot said it was too dangerous to land there, but a light further west indicated a safe place to land over there. Upon awakening, she realised that she didn't want to stay in Massachusetts, where she grew up, but wanted to go for a programme that would enable her to move away from home.

DO DREAMS SOLVE OUR PROBLEMS? (SPOILER: NO)

In this example, and in most of the others, it wasn't just the dream itself that was needed, because the dream didn't exactly offer a clear-cut solution. The waking mind was needed as well to figure out what the dream meant in relation to the problem. Remember Kekulé: the dream didn't tell him the chemical structure of benzene is a circle; it showed him an ouroboros, which is circular shaped. It took both the dream and the waking mind working together to come up with the insight. Dreams may picture things we are indecisive about or confused over, but the solution doesn't usually come neatly packaged in the dream; rather, we need to recall the dream and think about the problem more the next day to find the insight.

In terms of possible functions of dreaming, so far in this chapter we've talked mainly about how dreams reflect waking life: our memories in the first section, our emotions in the second, and now our problems or things on which we're working. But dreams, of course, are not merely mirrors of waking life; they are so much more than that. When we go to sleep, something truly magical happens: we create dreams, and dreams are almost always a work of intense imagination. Sometimes dreams are so creative, and so unlike waking life, that we struggle even to put them into words.

This, then, appears to be closer to the mark than the theory that dreams solve problems: dreams are works of extraordinary creativity, and this creative work helps us in many ways when we're awake. One of the things it does is presents our problems or things we're working on in strange, metaphorical, or otherwise creative ways. And if we take time to think about those dreams, and continue working on the problem in waking life, the dream and our waking minds together may come up with something insightful when they work in harmony like this.

DREAM RECALL AND CREATIVITY: WHAT'S THE LINK?

We also know that people with a particularly rich dream life are also particularly creative; for example, people who recall their dreams often tend to do well at various creative tasks. They also have other traits related to creativity, such as 'thin boundaries' (seeing the world as fluid and multifaceted, in 'shades of grey') rather than 'thick boundaries' (seeing the world through dichotomies, i.e. in 'black or white'), and they score high in the personality trait 'openness to experience'.

An experiment in 2019 by Mauricio Sierra-Siegert and his colleagues made the links between dream recall and creativity even clearer. He came up with a method to increase dream recall, and asked half of his participants to do this, while the other half didn't. The method was very simple: they were asked to think about whether they had had a dream each morning when they awoke, for a month. Both before and afterwards, participants also took tests of creativity. The method worked: not only did the first group recall way more dreams, but they also improved on some of their creativity scores. This shows that by simply paying more attention to our dreams, we can increase both our recall and our creativity.

SIMULATION THEORIES

DREAMING FOR THE FUTURE

So far, we've talked mostly about dreaming having potential functions in terms of dealing with experiences we've already had: remembering experiences, dealing with emotions, solving problems. But dreaming isn't all about the past. In fact, in one study I conducted, I found that participants mainly rated dreams as 'important' to them if they pertained to their future, not to their past. Perhaps this could be another function of dreams then: preparing us for the future?

I often dream of things for which I need to prepare, and I bet you do too. I wouldn't even like to guess how many hours I've spent panicking in dreams because I've turned up late or forgotten to prepare for a class I'm teaching. But I have literally never experienced this in waking life – I have never failed to prepare for a class, and I've never missed one by accident, or even arrived late – so this can't be a memory that I'm consolidating or a horrible past experience I'm trying to process.

Instead, maybe it's reminding me that this is important, so I need to be ready for it. Maybe a reason that I haven't ever accidentally missed a class or forgotten to prepare is because my dreams won't let me forget! And as much as I hate those dreams, I have to admit that if that's what they're doing, I appreciate them; I'd rather dream of embarrassing myself like this in front my students than do so in waking life!

In this section, we'll take a look at a few different dream theories that speculate about this aspect of dreams: that maybe dreams are simulating our reality for us so that we can prepare for it.

THE THREAT SIMULATION THEORY

The earliest of these simulation theories is the Threat Simulation Theory (TST), put forward by Finnish oneirologist Antti Revonsuo in 2000. Unlike my dreams of missing a class, this theory deals with the more physically dangerous, existential threats we sometimes have to deal with in dreams.

Cast your mind back to the last time that you were chased by something in a dream – by wolves, zombies, aliens, or just a bunch of angry people – and remember how you felt and what you did. Probably your fight-or-flight response kicked in during the dream, you felt intense fear, felt your body pumped full of adrenaline and noradrenaline, and you ran like crazy to get away.

Now, what would you do in waking life if you were chased by creatures that mean you harm? Exactly the same thing? The Threat Simulation Theory comes from the idea that dreams immerse us in threatening scenarios, and this helps us to rehearse what to do in those situations. Dreaming of being chased, for example, is the number one most common dream. Other common dreams involve natural or other disasters, or strangers meaning us harm. In these dreams, we often try to escape, run, or fight, as we would in waking life.

Threat Simulation Theory comes from an evolutionary psychology perspective. It says that when most of the humans living on earth were hunter-gatherers, threats to physical safety were much more common than they are now to people living in industrialised societies, and so having a mechanism that helped us to rehearse how to avoid such physical threats would be beneficial for survival. That mechanism, it was suggested, is dreaming, and it lingers today because our move away from small hunter-gatherer societies into enormous industrialised societies is so phylogenetically recent that the mechanism remains as it did when it evolved in our ancestors. And besides, we still dream about plenty of threats that are of concern to us. Being chased is still, obviously, something that can and does happen to some people in modern life, and other, more common modern threats include things like threats to livelihood.

ANXIETY DREAMS: ARE THEY PREPARING US FOR MODERN THREATS?

Let's go back to my work-related anxiety dreams for a moment. A similar kind of dream is often experienced by people who have been through a typical school education that puts a great deal of pressure on students to pass exams: that awful dream that you're in an exam situation and you've forgotten to prepare, or gone to the wrong exam, or never knew there was an exam in the first place. Remember I mentioned that being chased is a very common dream? So is failing an exam. In one study, almost half of all the participants surveyed reported having had an exam-related dream. Do dreams protect us from these kinds of threats?

Several studies have investigated exam dreams. Isabelle Arnulf and her colleagues in France, were intrigued by the idea that failing an exam in a dream could lead to success in the exam in waking life. Students who reported dreaming of the exam the night before they sat it attained higher grades than those who did not, and it didn't matter what kind of dream they had: whether the exam dream was pleasant or unpleasant, whether it was long or short, bizarre or mundane, and whether it pictured being ill, poor preparation, being late, or whatever – none of the characteristics of the dream led to different outcomes in grade. As long as they recalled dreaming of the exam, they performed better at it. Perhaps just like me and my 'being unprepared for my class' dreams, these exam-anxiety dreams are motivating because they instil fear of failure. (Or, then again, maybe it's just that more conscientious students dream more of exams.)

THE SOCIAL SIMULATION THEORY

It's curious that when I have anxiety dreams about work, they always revolve around the same theme, which is screwing up a class I'm meant to be teaching. But teaching is only one aspect of my work, and I don't tend to have anxiety dreams about the other aspects: I rarely dream about applying for funding, running experiments, or marking student papers, yet these aspects of my work can all cause me anxiety in waking life too. Why is it that I dream only of teaching worries and none of the others?

There is something that is true for teaching anxiety that is not true for other work anxieties: when I give a class lecture, it is essentially a performance – in front of students most of the time, in front of peers if it is at a conference, or in front of the general public if I'm giving a public talk. This means there is the possibility of social embarrassment: if I mess up when I'm giving a talk, people are watching me mess up, whereas if I mess up in any of the other things I do at work, it might be stressful but it's not in front of a room full of people. That, I think, is perhaps why I dream so often of that work anxiety and less so about others: the fear of social embarrassment.

And perhaps social embarrassment is, in fact, a kind of ancestral threat. Humans are social creatures and have evolved to live in communities. Being accepted into or rejected by a community could well be the difference between surviving and thriving on the one hand and scraping together a meagre existence or dying on the other. If we have evolved embarrassment to tell us when we're doing something that our group won't like and will cause them to reject us, this would be beneficial in terms of knowing how to behave to be accepted into the group.

From such ideas was born a second simulation theory, again from Antti Revonsuo, called the Social Simulation Theory (SST). This theory is derived from evolutionary theories about the sociability of humankind and how this sociability has helped us in the evolutionary race. Evidence for this theory comes partly from the obvious fact that the dreaming world is enormously sociable. In the dreams of some college students in the USA, they were alone in only around 5% of their dreams (Domhoff, 1996). In the rest, most of the other characters are humans (some familiar, some strangers), and there may also be non-human animals. Dreaming has been shown to be even more social than waking, and the appearance of waking-life people in dreams is determined by how much time we've spent with them and how close they are to us.

DREAMING AS PLAY

A criticism that has been levelled against simulation or rehearsal theories is the fact that dreaming can be very weird. Many things happen in dreams that either would not or could not happen in waking life. If we are really rehearsing skills that would be helpful in the future, why is the dream world so unlike the waking world? Plus, we often don't seem to be rehearsing any kind of realistic threat or social situation, and even if the situation was realistic, the outcome might not be very helpful. Threats we can't escape from in a dream, for example, like being caught by the creatures chasing us, or being caught up in a natural disaster that is inescapable: it's hard to see how this would be helpful to rehearse.

Why is dreaming so weird then? One idea comes from oneirologist Kelly Bulkeley, which agrees with other simulation theories that dreaming is a virtual world in which we explore and experiment. But what makes his idea different is that he sees dreaming less like rehearsal and more like play – the kind of recreational, imaginative playing we did as children.

He notes many crossovers between dreaming and play: both are 'autotelic' (they are done 'just because', there is no specific goal); they are done in a safe, fictional environment (even though the subject might be dangerous); they often have strong emotions associated with them, both pleasant and unpleasant; they may be bizarre or absolutely nonsensical; they often draw material from genuine concerns from waking life, especially our own survival; they are often extravagant and exaggerated; they deviate from the normal rules governing waking life, and so they allow for experimentation.

And just as the features of dreaming and playing are related, so might their functions be: for example, they both allow the individual to explore and experiment with a wide range of possibilities and to practice ways of behaving in and experiencing a fictional world that is like the 'real' world; they promote creative thinking; they enable us to interact with others and take on different social roles, which may promote empathy; they help us to learn our own cultural norms. Perhaps there are many other functions too.

Unlike the others, the 'dreaming is play' theory allows for 'the multiplicity of dreams' – not just threatening, sociable, or other specific kinds of dreams, but many different types of dreams. This approach can actually subsume the other theories, and it also answers the question of why dreams can be so weird: dreams are "a playful expression of the creative imagination".

The idea that dreaming involves a simulation of the waking world through playful, creative exploration is attractive because it does not presume a singular function of dreaming any more than it proposes that dreaming is itself singular. Play may have any number of functions and outcomes, but it also may result in accidents and unpleasant experiences, just as dreaming does.

Many dream theories fall down when confronted with some of the worst kinds of dreaming, especially the nightmares experienced by PTSD sufferers, because it's hard to see how dreams that repeatedly replay traumatic experiences can be helpful. In fact, these dreams can be re-traumatising, because they force the person to relive their worst memories. To explain these, Bulkeley says that they are a "violent interruption of the capacity to play within the space of dreaming". This makes a lot of sense: imagination is severely compromised in people with PTSD. For example, in his book *The Body Keeps the Score*, PTSD expert Bessel van der Kolk illustrates this with an experiment in which PTSD patients were asked to look at the Rorschach test pictures – those ambiguous inkblots on white paper. While people who didn't have PTSD interpreted the blobs in various imaginative ways, those with PTSD saw nothing but their own traumatic experiences in them. (We'll talk more about PTSD nightmares in Chapter 4.)

HOW DOES ALL THIS HAPPEN?

We have looked at four potential explanations of why we dream: to consolidate memories, to process emotions, to think creatively, and to simulate waking reality and 'play' with it. But what is it about dreams that enables any of these things to happen? In this final section, I will discuss two qualities of dreams that I think make the dream-state the perfect place for these processes to happen. These are dream *metaphor* and dream *hyperassociativity*. I will talk about each of these terms separately, but they are closely related.

METAPHOR

The first quality of the dream-state that makes it a fertile place for the various processes we've discussed is 'metaphoricity' – the quality of making metaphors. In general terms, a metaphor is any kind of non-literal relationship between two things; it is understanding one thing in terms of something else.

When you hear the word 'metaphor', perhaps you think of poetry. For many people, their first encounter with the word 'metaphor' is in literature classes at school. And metaphor is indeed often used in literature; Shakespeare, for example, used metaphor extensively to create beautiful language, like, "But Soft! What light through yonder window breaks? It is the East, and Juliet is the sun!" (from *Romeo and Juliet*), or to give new meaning to something, like "All the world's a stage, and all the men and women merely players" (from *As You Like It*).

But metaphor is by no means limited to literature. We use metaphor constantly in our lives, often without even realising it. Much of our everyday language is based on metaphor: we use it to understand our thoughts and feelings. For example, the phrases "I'm on top of the world!" and "I'm on cloud nine!" mean "I feel good"; but "I feel pretty low" and "I'm down in the dumps" mean "I feel bad". Other examples of everyday metaphor are innumerable: "You're barking up the wrong tree", "She's under the weather", and so on. We use metaphor so often we probably don't even think of it as metaphor.

Dreams also use metaphor to express abstract concepts and feelings. But whereas language is verbal, dreams are visual and embodied: whereas metaphor in literature is written, metaphor in dreams is seen and experienced. But we're not talking about the kind of Freudian symbolism we explored in Chapter 2. A cigar in your dream is (probably) not a phallic symbol. A banana in your dream is (probably) not a phallic symbol. A gun in your dream is (probably) not a phallic symbol. In fact, most things in your dreams are probably not phallic symbols. Dreams often deal with things that we consider to be important from waking life, so if sex is really important to someone, then they probably do dream about it often; but unless you think about phalluses all day every day (maybe you do; I'm not here to judge), then it's unlikely that your dreams are brimming with phallic or other sexual symbols.[5]

Metaphor is not universal; it is influenced by the individual's culture, beliefs, and understandings of the world. We share some metaphors, others may be unique to us, and yet others may be both shared and individualised. Let's take an example. Research by Kelly Bulkeley suggests that in palliative care patients – people nearing the end of their life – dreams of journeys are very common, and these 'journey dreams' may symbolise the journey towards death. But for each patient, the dream journey will be unique to them and can only be understood in light of what they believe, think, worry about, want, have experienced, and so on.

Most oneirologists agree that dreams can be metaphorical for waking life. Despite this, there's very little in the way of psychological research on this topic because it's very tricky to approach. Why? Well, let's say I dream about standing on a beach while a tidal wave approaches and then engulfs me. I wake up and think that the dream is a metaphor for me feeling overwhelmed at work. How do I know that's the 'right' interpretation of the dream? It could also be interpreted as a threat simulation dream, or a distorted memory of being engulfed by a large wave at the beach as a child, or a dream that pictures fears about the effects of climate change. Trying to understand what a dream is metaphorical for, or indeed if it is metaphorical at all, is an inherently subjective process, and there is no way to check the 'right' interpretation.

Similarly, dream metaphors may be obscured by the fact that the metaphor in the dream could be something you experienced years ago in your waking life. Let's return to that common dream, the exam dream. If you are about to take an exam, dreaming about this is hardly surprising. But what if you have this dream and you haven't taken an exam in years and never will again? Many people tell me this is the case for them, and oneirologist Antonio Zadra (1996) documented exactly this. A woman first dreamt about turning up unprepared to an exam when she was 19 years old, in college, so this was a real waking-life worry for her then. After she graduated, she stopped having the dreams. But years later she began to have the dream again every week in the months leading up to her wedding. It was as if the stress and anxiety of the wedding made her dreams associate back to the stress and anxiety of exams, and so the exam dreams became a kind of metaphorical representation of her present-day stress.

It's commonly believed that emotion is what drives metaphor generation in dreams. In the example presented earlier, it's stress and anxiety that create a bridge between the two otherwise unrelated experiences: taking exams and getting married. In this way, we could say that the stress of getting married *associated* to examination stress. This idea of dream metaphors being associations between two things brings us to the second quality of dreams: hyperassociativity.

HYPERASSOCIATIVITY

WAKE-DREAM HYPERASSOCIATIVITY

In the previous section, we saw how a dream about something from our past can become a metaphor for something in our present if they both bring about the same emotions, such as feelings of stress or anxiety. We saw that it looks like the waking-life situation (e.g. wedding) *associates* to something from one's past with the same emotions (e.g. exams) in the dream.

Sometimes this association can be between two closely related things. If you were taking an exam and dreamt of taking an exam, the waking-life situation and the dream would be very closely related. But if you were getting married and dreamt of taking an exam, the association would be much more distant. Another way we could describe a distant association is that it is a *hyper*association.

Oneirologist Bill Domhoff (1993) gave another example of this kind. He found that American veterans of the Vietnam War dreamt often of their wartime experiences. Over time, they eventually stopped having these dreams. But decades later, they began dreaming of it again when they were up against something stressful in their waking life – like marital difficulties. Just as the woman dreamt of taking an exam when she was about to get married because both events brought about feelings of stress, so the veterans dreamt of the war again when their current lives were stressful.

This shows how post-traumatic nightmares can re-emerge years after trauma if something that's somehow related to the trauma comes up, even if the relation is very distant. This is why people now use 'trigger warnings' for upsetting information or images, because for people with experience of trauma, it can have real consequences, like re-emergence of traumatic nightmares.

Let's look at one more example, this time from a psychology experiment (Davidson & Lynch, 2012). Half of the participants watched a video about the 9/11 atrocities, and the other half watched a psychology lecture video. That night, they recorded their dreams. The researchers wanted to know whether watching a video about 9/11 would give them dreams of it, but they didn't only look for close references to the 9/11 video, like dreaming of a plane crashing into the Twin Towers; they also looked for more distantly related content, like any kind of crash. Not only did the 9/11 group dream more of directly related images than the psychology lecture group, but also of those more distantly associated images as well.

These examples all show that experiencing something in waking life can bring about very loosely associated, or hyperassociated, content in dreams.

DREAM-DREAM HYPERASSOCIATIVITY

So far, we've looked at hyperassociativity between a waking event (e.g. a wedding) and the subsequent dream content it hyperassociates to (e.g. taking an exam). Another kind of hyperassociativity happens within the dream itself. It's a common feature of dreams that things change very suddenly. One moment you're talking to a character who is the woman who lives next door, and the next minute she's your mother. Likewise, dreams often change scene suddenly – one minute you're in your family home; the next minute you're in an unfamiliar mansion. One study found that over three-quarters of dreams contain these kinds of abrupt changes within the dream narrative. Sometimes places or people will even be two or more things simultaneously – the character is both the old woman next door and your mother; the location is both your family home and an unfamiliar mansion.

Likewise, another common feature in dreams is that you'll find various unrelated or only very distantly related things from your waking life all jumbled together. Your mother is in the dream, but so is your university tutor *and* a character from the TV show you watched last night. In this way, dreams pluck extremely different memories and concepts from our waking lives and mix them all together, chopping and changing constantly, blending things we recognise from our waking lives with things that we don't recognise, often in ways that seem bizarre and unrealistic to our waking-life minds. Here's a dream of mine as an illustration of dream hyperassociativity.

> There are some students in the corridor where my office is. I'm meant to be meeting up with them and talking to them about their dissertations. I'm really late. They're doing something about performance arts, dreams, and stroke survivors. This is S__'s project. Next to them there's another student, who looks a bit like my brother. I think about how maybe there are just generational iterations of people who look the same, but aren't necessarily related. His name was C__, and he looked also a bit like my cousin, who is called C__. The students were singing this song about how their ancestors lived in the Forest of Dean and the Island of Babylon. I was sitting there feeling very sceptical, thinking, 'how could you possibly know that?' It was painful to listen to because they had awful singing voices.

In this dream, I can pick out at least ten clear crossovers between the dream and my waking life: 1) my upcoming meeting with students; 2) my anxiety about being late; 3) my friend who teaches art classes to stroke survivors; 4) my colleague S__ with whom I had been talking about dream projects; 5) my brother; 6) my cousin; 7) an event I was going to in Glastonbury in the near future (which the dream changed to the Forest of Dean); 8) the song 'Gates of Babylon' by Rainbow; 9) my sceptical mindset; 10) the fact that I have a rubbish singing voice (and was contemplating public singing).

As you can see, in one very short dream scene, there are many different elements of my life, some of which are clearly related to each other (e.g. my brother and my cousin) but others that are not really related at all, and it's not obvious why the dream would squish them all together (e.g. my brother and my work colleague). As well as throwing all these distantly related or perhaps even unrelated aspects of my waking life together, the dream is also varied in terms of the time period in my life to which it refers. It goes all the way back to childhood memories, through to the present day and off into the future. It's hyperassociative because it's associating between various elements of my waking life in an extremely loose ('hyper') way.

Although I have discussed metaphor and hyperassociativity separately, I'm not suggesting that there are metaphorical dreams on the one hand and hyperassociative dreams on the other. Dreams are often complex, messy, bizarre, and confusing, and may encapsulate metaphorical imagery and hyperassociativity at the same time. Plus, the two concepts are related: being stressed in waking life might hyperassociate to examination stress and so give you an exam dream; this would be both a hyperassociation and could be seen also as a metaphor.

LONG LIVE IMAGINATION!

The big question, then, is why? Why are dreams metaphorical and hyperassociative?

The crux of it is imagination. Both metaphor and hyperassociativity, as well as other qualities of dreams like their bizarreness, are aspects of the dreaming brain's extraordinary ability to imagine new things, odd things, surprising things. This imaginative quality of dreaming may be exactly what our sleeping brains need to consolidate memories, process emotions, think creatively, and simulate and play with waking reality.

Dreams do this in a way our waking minds just can't. When we're awake, most of the time we have to deal with incoming information from the external world: phones ringing, people talking, paying attention in class, eating breakfast, and so on; we're constantly bombarded with things 'out there' in the world we need to do or respond to. Even when we're daydreaming, we still need to make sure we're not ignoring someone or getting run over as we cross the street. But when we go to sleep, we are cut off from that world, and our minds can roam freely.

And they really do! Dreams are extraordinary feats of imagination and creation in ways that our waking minds can scarcely comprehend. Creating new metaphors and making hyperassociations are just two aspects of their intense imaginativeness.

Metaphors, for example, create something more than the sum of their parts. Metaphors breathe new life and new meaning into ideas we already hold. In Shakespeare's line "But Soft! What light through yonder window breaks? It is the East, and Juliet is the sun!", this metaphor gives us a new sense of Juliet's beauty and of Romeo's adoration of her. But it does more than that: it is also emotional, powerful, and beautiful. Dream metaphors can be like this too: they can give us new understandings, and they, too, can be emotional, powerful, beautiful (or terrible).

Hyperassociations can achieve the same by making associations between two things that might not have been associated before. Oneirologist Ernest Hartmann provided an example of this: he said, imagine someone dreamt that their father and boyfriend were the same person. At first when they wake up, they might feel disgust; but later on, when they see their boyfriend again, they realise: "Oh no; he *is* just like my father!" This is a very simple example to illustrate the idea, but most dreams are likely to do this in much more complex and dense ways.

Dream metaphor and dream hyperassociativity tie together the four functional interpretations of dreaming discussed earlier: memory consolidation, emotion-processing, creativity, and simulation/play. We dream of our present, past, and anticipated future experiences in bizarre, metaphorical, and hyperassociative ways, and this helps us to make sense of our world, comparing past experiences with present ones, making very wide comparisons between seemingly unrelated memories and experiences, and experiencing them as reality.

If we remind ourselves of the evidence we've already encountered, it starts to make sense. Recall in the memory consolidation section that although dreaming of newly acquired memories led to better recall of them, the dreams people had didn't seem to make sense – they were not dreaming of the exact experience – running through a virtual maze, perhaps – but of only very distantly related memories or images, such as a maze-like bat cave they'd once been to. Something about this hyperassociation from the new memory to something distantly related led to better memory consolidation.

Or recall that when Rosalind Cartwright looked at the dreams of divorcees, she found that the divorcees who didn't develop depression had dreams with lots of time variance (i.e. dreams that pictured the past, present, and future altogether). This is a type of hyperassociativity. In contrast, the divorcees who ended up with depression did not have hyperassociative dreams. This shows that people who dream hyperassociatively are also better at coping with emotional experiences.

And creativity? Well, many sleep experiments have now shown that we are at our most insightful following a period of REM sleep, which is when we have our most bizarre and our most metaphorical and hyperassociative dreams. Perhaps this shows that metaphor and hyperassociativity during sleep are what underlie those creative juices flowing after a REM period. Overnight, information we have acquired and stored is reconfigured in novel ways, fusing formerly separate elements together to generate that eureka! moment, or, more subtly, slowly and gradually shifting us towards new ways of thinking about old problems and past experiences. Metaphors, too, can themselves give insights: Kekulé's ouroboros was a metaphorical representation of the circular structure of benzene.

Let's not forget simulation and play: it may be crucial that dreams are not just images that we see but experiences that we live in for them to have the effects that they do. We inhabit a virtual reality, composed of our jumbled-up memories and experiences, sometimes in metaphorical ways, and this has real-world effects on the ways that we think and behave.

Some people wonder, but how can these dreams be functional if we don't even remember most of them? And the answer is that we don't have to always be consciously aware of this process for it to be beneficial. There are many adaptive processes that we are not consciously aware of all the time. Take language as an example. We learn the rules of language as children without even knowing we're doing so. Or memory consolidation, as another. We strengthen our memories while we sleep without even trying to. So there's no reason to suppose that the adaptive benefits of dreaming only happen if we recall the dream. We may be able to get *even more* from the dream process by recalling and then working more with dreams whilst awake, but if we want to argue that they are adaptive, then it shouldn't be necessary to recall them for this.

In this chapter we've spoken much about how dreams relate to our waking lives. But this is only one part of dreaming. Dreams are nothing like our waking lives sometimes; they are suffused with oneiric dark matter: we don't really know what it is, but it's holding the whole dream together. People we haven't met, places we haven't been to, experiences we've never had. The dream is always a novel creation, it's often bizarre, and it's often very different from waking life. This is all part of the hypothesised process that I'm describing; the dream is a feat of intense imaginative abilities, a force of creativity, the likes of which most of us could not produce with waking consciousness. Dreams create beauty, absurdity, bizarreness, and horror in the most masterful ways. It's no wonder that they are such a source of inspiration to inventors, artists, poets, novelists, and the like, and we are beginning to understand how they might be essential to waking life in many other ways too.

'THE' FUNCTION OF DREAMING?

It seems pointless to argue about 'the' function of dreaming, when dreaming is such a diverse phenomenon. If dreaming is a conscious experience during sleep, then it is bound to be as multifaceted as waking consciousness. With such a range of dreams existing, how can we suggest that there is *a* function, and then try to find it by pigeon-holing all dream experiences into this one function? It seems more sensible and likely that dreaming serves many functions, and in some cases, no function; in fact, in other cases, dreaming may well be malfunctional, as we will see in the next section with traumatic nightmares.

4

DREAMING AND MENTAL HEALTH

DEPRESSION, TRAUMA, AND PSYCHOSIS

The relationship between sleeping and mental health is very well-known, so much so that many of the diagnoses set out in the *Diagnostic and Statistical Manual of Mental Disorders*[1] include 'sleep disturbances' as a symptom. For example, the diagnoses of depression, anxiety disorders, bipolar disorder, and post-traumatic stress disorder all include sleep disturbances as possible symptoms.

Similarly, it's well established that nightmares and other kinds of bad dreams may occur during times of stress, poor mental health, and following trauma. During periods of depression, dreams often relate to difficult life circumstances that contribute to or cause the depression, as we saw in Chapter 3. We will look at depression briefly in this chapter; if you would like to know more about dreams and depression, Rosalind Cartwright's book discusses this in greater detail. More space in this chapter will be given to two specific topics in dreams and mental health, topics which have very clear relevance for oneirology: trauma (and its associated effects on mental health) and psychosis (or 'schizophrenia'). Trauma, and especially the disorder that may follow trauma (PTSD), may lead to a huge change in dream content, causing traumatic nightmares to occur; and psychosis has a long history of being considered a kind of 'waking dream' state. But first, let's look briefly at what is currently known about dreaming and depression.[2]

DEPRESSION

When it comes to depression and sleep, the research is clear: sleep disturbance is not just a symptom of depression but may also precede it. A meta-analysis (huge analysis of the results of many experiments all together) found that if a person without depression has insomnia, they are twice as likely to become depressed later on than if they didn't have insomnia. If you get people into a lab and stop them from sleeping (a bit cruel, but useful for understanding sleep and only with their informed consent), their mood will get steadily worse and worse the more deprived of sleep they are. So if sleep isn't going well, depression may follow.

Once in a period of depression, sleep doesn't improve: some people experience insomnia in depression, and others go in the opposite direction and develop hypersomnia (over-sleeping). People with depression also have an overabundance of REM sleep. Their REM sleep periods are longer, denser (more eye movements), and occur earlier in the night. Coupled with this, they get less Stage 3 sleep. So depression deprives the sufferer of the lovely physically healing Stage 3 sleep and also gives them too much of the hyper-emotional REM sleep.

And dreams are also different in depression. Depressed people tend to have dreams with more negative emotions than others or have dreams that are flat and unemotional. This likely follows on from waking-life symptoms: either feeling very unpleasant emotions or not feeling very much of anything at all. But successful treatment of depression with medication reverses this: for example, one study found that after eight weeks of taking antidepressants, a group of depressed individuals who were beginning to improve began to recall more dreams and have generally more pleasant dreams (Quartini, 2014).

Cartwright's work with people going through divorce shed further light on the relationship between dreams and recovery from depression (see Chapter 3).

A model of how depression works suggests that during the day, a depressed person pays more attention to unpleasant feelings and experiences and then replays these feelings and experiences at night during sleep (Harrington et al., 2017). In this way, depression is like a vicious cycle: we see our waking life as unpleasant, so we go to bed with a low mood; then we dream about these unpleasant feelings, so we wake up with a low mood too. To break the cycle, some kind of intervention may be needed, whether that comes in the form of medicine, talking therapy, or something else.

TRAUMATIC NIGHTMARES AND PTSD

We know from the previous chapter that dreams replay memories from waking life in bizarre, sometimes hyperassociative, and sometimes metaphorical ways, and that this probably serves many different functions. But it's not always this neat and tidy. Sometimes the process gets completely thrown out of whack. Sometimes dreams become nightmares.

We saw in Chapter 3 that nightmares aren't all bad. But sometimes they can become *really* bad, not only because they are distressing to experience but also because sometimes they are not helping us process emotional experiences but may actually be making us feel *worse*. This is particularly the case in the kind of nightmare that replays over and over again, never really changing, just invading sleep and haunting dreams, making the dreamer scared to go to bed for fear of experiencing it yet again.

These kinds of nightmares follow from traumatic experiences, which range from extremely serious events that endanger life, safety, and bodily integrity – like war, sexual assault and abuse, physical violence, persecution, vehicular accidents, and natural disasters – to those more commonly experienced as part of a normal life cycle, such as bereavement and separation.

Trauma doesn't affect everyone the same way. For some people, it is possible to recover and to continue with life without the event having a major impact on their lives afterwards. Some may even experience post-traumatic growth: to adapt in such a way that subsequent living is improved, perhaps in terms of having a greater appreciation for life. But for others, post-trauma life can become a literal nightmare. Post-traumatic stress disorder (PTSD) may follow trauma for some, and this is very often accompanied by frequent, incredibly distressing nightmares.

A MALFUNCTION OF THE DREAMING PROCESS

Both Freud and Jung saw traumatic nightmares as exceptions to the 'normal' dreaming process. After the First World War, when many returning soldiers brought 'shell shock' (now known as PTSD) home, Freud perceived that the traumatic nightmares they were experiencing were not wish-fulfilments and therefore were outside of the 'ordinary' spectrum of dreaming. Instead, he considered these kinds of dreams to be part of what he called the "repetition compulsion", in which a person returns repeatedly to a traumatising experience in order to try and come to terms with it. Similarly, Jung (2002) wrote that the traumatic nightmare, "which is essentially only a reproduction of the trauma", is not compensatory and so did not fit with his conceptualisation of dream function. A similar sentiment is echoed now, in the sense that oneirologists still see traumatic nightmares as a malfunction of the typical dreaming process.

The kind of nightmares that are produced by traumatic experiences are unlike most dreams in that they replay an experience from waking life over and over again, often almost exactly as it originally happened. We have seen (in Chapter 3) that while dream content is often drawn from various parts of our waking lives, dreams only very rarely replay an experience exactly as it happened. Even 'normal' nightmares are unlike traumatic nightmares – they're much scarier than dreams, but they still don't reproduce actual waking-life experiences in their entirety. But post-traumatic nightmares are stuck in replication, and unlike dreams and other kinds of nightmares, they are not hyperassociative, which, as we've seen, may be one of the key qualities of dreaming that helps us to process emotional experiences (see Chapter 3).

THE MORE SEVERE THE TRAUMA, THE MORE DIRECT THE NIGHTMARE

There is an association between the severity of a traumatic experience and the effect it has on dreaming. Some of the most extreme examples come from the post-traumatic nightmares of American soldiers returning from the Vietnam War who had variously committed and/or witnessed atrocities, were exposed to extreme danger to their lives, experienced intense, prolonged fear, were often badly injured, and saw the pain and suffering caused by the war both to their friends and to the people of Vietnam. It is unsurprising, then, that many of the surviving men were severely traumatised when they returned home.

The veterans of the Vietnam War were of course not the first people to return from war with trauma, but it was after this war that the new diagnosis of PTSD was added to the *Diagnostic and Statistical Manual of Mental Disorders*. This was needed because of the public response to traumatised veterans. They were often viewed with suspicion (they weren't 'really' ill), with disdain (they were 'weak'), and with fear (they were 'dangerous'). The new term 'PTSD' gave a mental health diagnosis to a group who had experienced extreme trauma and whose behaviour changed in direct response to those experiences. And the dreams of the veterans with PTSD were often exact replays of terrible experiences they had had during the war.

Conversely, when an individual has a traumatic experience of war but as a civilian rather than as a combatant, post-traumatic dreams tend to be different. Research with Dutch veterans and civilians of World War II, who developed PTSD either from combat experience or having been subject to occupation, found that while veterans and civilians experienced post-traumatic nightmares with similar frequency, the content of those nightmares differed (Schreuder et al., 1998). The veterans, just like the Vietnam veterans, tended to have replicative nightmares that depicted actual experiences from combat. Civilians who had experienced occupation, however, tended to have more dream-like nightmares that didn't necessarily depict actual events but were nevertheless terrifying. This is because they each had different experiences: while both groups witnessed atrocities, veterans experienced more danger to their own lives and witnessed more atrocities and more death. This shows that the directness with which dreams portray traumatic events is dependent on the extent of the trauma and the extent of personal exposure to death and danger.

Further evidence for this idea comes from a study led by Raija-Leena Punamäki at the University of Tampere in Finland. Her research group studied Kurdish children who had been living in Iraq during the reign of Saddam Hussein and whose families had been persecuted by his regime. Many of the children had been orphaned, and all had grown up during years of massacre, persecution, and ethnic cleansing. The children with the most personal experience of trauma such as witnessing violence, being separated from family, or suffering hardships such as hunger, had the most unpleasant and the most nightmarish dreams. Among the children with high levels of personal traumatic experiences, those who had pleasant, complex dreams had less psychological distress. It's possible that this indicates a protective, healing function of these dreams, in keeping with our discussions of dream function in the previous chapter.

Several other studies have confirmed these findings. In one US-based study, dreams of children who attended an elementary school at which there was a sniper attack in the playground were studied (Pynoos et al., 1987). Two-thirds of the children who were actually in the playground at the time of the attack had traumatic nightmares about it; just over half who were in school but not on the playground had traumatic nightmares; just under half of those who were not at school that day had them; and a third of children who were on vacation at the time had them. This pattern clearly shows that the closer the children were to danger the more likely they were to have traumatic nightmares about it.

AS THE TRAUMA HEALS, THE NIGHTMARE CHANGES

Continuing along this path, the directness with which a person dreams of their trauma is also associated with their stage of recovery.

Psychiatrist Harry Wilmer also treated men returning from the Vietnam War. He found that the content of their nightmares came in three forms. In the first form, which he called 'Actual', the nightmares replicated usually the most traumatic experience from the war, like being attacked, seeing children killed, or seeing friends killed. The second form of nightmare, the 'Variable' nightmare, depicted plausible war scenarios but didn't replicate something that had actually happened. Sometimes the nightmare was set completely in Vietnam, but sometimes it would weave in elements from their current waking life. In the third form of nightmare, the 'Hallucinatory' nightmare, there would be some identification with the war in the dream, but it would otherwise be more like an 'ordinary' nightmare, very often referring to current waking life as well as the war. These three types of nightmares existed on a healing continuum: as the veteran moved from Actual replicative nightmares, through Variable nightmares, and towards Hallucinatory nightmares, so they began to heal and integrate and come to terms with the horrors they experienced.

A similar pattern of healing was documented by Johanna King and Jacqueline Sheehan, who worked with survivors of childhood incest. They found that there were different stages of dream content that the survivors experienced – not necessarily in a completely linear direction, but usually in roughly the same way. First, when the survivor is completely unable to accept what happened, self-defence mechanisms of denial and repression operate. In this stage, dreams may depict hiding, avoiding, or refusing to see. Then, acknowledgment of the abuse plays out in dreams: they replay the experience, often exactly as it happened, or they depict the effects of the abuse (e.g. paralysis and terror). After some time, dreams move towards growth and understanding: they may depict the survivor realising they weren't to blame and could not have prevented the abuse. Eventually, the survivor reaches the renegotiation stage, where they are able to come to terms with what happened to them and move on. In this stage, the survivors may dream of getting revenge, setting boundaries, or protecting themselves.

We can see, then, that as healing and recovery take place, nightmare content changes. Depending on the kind of trauma experienced, it may begin as a replicative nightmare and gradually change to an ordinary nightmare and eventually an ordinary dream, or it may begin as a repression of the content in the form of hiding nightmares and gradually change to accepting and recovering types of dreams. Delineating these stages of traumatic dreaming can therefore be helpful for clinicians to understand where their patients are in the recovery process.

THE CONTINUUM OF TRAUMATIC NIGHTMARES TO NORMAL DREAMING

Just as it's possible to trace the pattern from replicative nightmare to ordinary nightmare as healing occurs, so we can continue in this direction towards more regular types of dreaming that occur for the population at large. For example, everyone who lives an average lifespan is bound to experience bereavement at some point, and in dreams that follow bereavement the healing process can also be discerned. These stages have been traced out by Patricia Garfield.

Just as the response to traumas often begin with repression, so the response to bereavement often begins with denial. Dreams at this stage of bereavement may picture the dead alive again, with the death having been a mistake. Following this, disorganised, chaotic feelings follow, such as anxiety, sadness, anger, and, of course, grief. Dreams during this stage take many forms such as receiving a phone call from the deceased or watching them take a journey. The final stage is the acceptance stage, in which they may dream of receiving a gift or message from the deceased. These bereavement dream stages clearly parallel the stages of healing from trauma and the accompanying nightmares.

In this way, we can see that to some extent traumatic dreaming is not so different from regular dreaming after all. Several oneirologists have argued that we can see how much of an emotional impact an event has had by the extent to which dreams repeatedly picture the same experiences. It's most obvious following extreme trauma, in individuals who develop PTSD, in which the experience is repeatedly replayed just as it happened. But we can also see it in, for example, recurrent dreams, and in dreams that repeat the same themes (e.g. feelings of loneliness) or the same person (e.g. an old flame). These repetitions may indicate that there is something there that is unfinished or that we are still fixated on.

The continuum could even be extended to aspects of waking-life experiences that only crop up in a dream once and then vanish – they did not need to be repeated because they were so mundane in the first place as to not need to be replayed over and over again. The study by Raphael Vallat we first visited in the previous chapter found that the majority of 'day residue', elements from the day just before the dream occurs, are often very mundane – they pop up in the dream once and then never again.

REPRESSION: FRIEND OR FOE?

A common and understandable response to trauma is denial and repression – defence mechanisms first described by Freud. But whether this way of coping with trauma helps the survivor adapt to life is a matter that is still being debated; some research suggests a repressive coping style is helpful, and other research suggests it may be harmful.

On the 'helpful' side of the research is the work of Peretz Lavie and Hannah Kaminer, who studied Holocaust survivors: people who had survived Nazi concentration camps or who had spent the war in hideouts or on the run. About half of these individuals had adjusted to life well after their experiences, while the other half were not doing so well. Wanting to understand what made the difference between them, the researchers examined many different factors, including the kinds of dreams they had and what kinds of coping strategies they used. They found that the well-adjusted group had an overall repressive way of coping: they avoided talking about their experiences so much that their relatives didn't even know they had direct experience of the war, they had very low dream recall, and of the dreams they did remember, they tended to be not very complex or emotional.

Conversely, a more recent study with Holocaust survivors conducted by Wojciech Owczarski at the University of Gdańsk, Poland, found that there were many apparently therapeutic dreams the survivors had about their traumatic experiences in Auschwitz, including dreams that clearly weave in other aspects of their waking lives, like the 'Variable' or 'Hallucinatory' nightmares of Vietnam veterans – which, as we saw earlier, are indicative of integration and recovery. Some also argue that trying to deny and avoid one's traumatic experiences can backfire and lead to an intensification of intrusive memories and nightmares. Work on the dream rebound effect[3] supports such a hypothesis; it shows that attempts to suppress unpleasant thoughts can have the opposite effect of having more dreams about those thoughts.

So there is some evidence in favour of repression and some against it. We need to better understand the effects of repression on coping – this will be of great benefit to trauma survivors.

TREATMENT FOR TRAUMATIC NIGHTMARES

For some people, experiencing nightmares following a trauma can be a part of the natural healing process. But for others, the progression from replicative traumatic nightmare to ordinary nightmare and eventually to ordinary dreaming just does not occur. Instead, the replicative nightmare just keeps coming back, time and time again, not progressing, not healing, and in fact having a re-traumatising effect. Rosalind Cartwright (1992) said that for these individuals, dreams get stuck "like a needle in the groove of a scratched record". So, for those who are stuck in their nightmares, external assistance is needed to help them heal and move on.

There are plenty of treatments for the daytime symptoms of PTSD, many of which have a stack of evidence for their efficacy, such as certain types of antidepressants, and cognitive behavioural therapy

(CBT). But even when most PTSD symptoms are successfully treated with these methods, sleep disturbances and traumatic nightmares often continue. Because of this, treatments that specifically target sleep and nightmares are essential.

Until recently, it was recommended that PTSD nightmares could be treated pharmacologically with a drug called prazosin. This drug can treat high blood pressure, and it was also thought to be able to banish nightmares by reducing the levels of adrenaline in the body. However, a recent experiment found that prazosin does not improve sleep quality or reduce nightmares – as such, it is no longer recommended for this purpose (Raskind et al., 2018).

Fortunately, however, effective psychological treatments do exist. There are quite a few available, but the one most clearly evidenced is called Image Rehearsal Therapy (IRT). In IRT, the patient chooses a repetitive nightmare – not necessarily one that clearly pictures a traumatic experience but one with which they are able to work. They write it down, and then with their waking imagination, they change some aspect of it so that it's no longer terrifying or distressing and write this new dream script down. With this in mind, they then practice or rehearse this new non-threatening and non-frightening dream, with their imagination, for ten to 20 minutes per day.

The research for IRT is unequivocal – it works (Krakow & Zadra, 2006). Following a course of IRT, those suffering from nightmare disorder (with PTSD or not) have fewer disturbing nightmares and better sleep quality, and the effect is maintained long-term – even once the therapy has finished. Amazingly, it also reduces other symptoms of PTSD as well, those experienced during the daytime. How exactly this works is still unknown, but somehow, by changing a nightmare with waking imagination, PTSD sufferers can find relief from all of their symptoms.

A related therapeutic method, called Focusing Oriented Dreamwork (FOD), also has patients re-imagining their nightmares and changing them in some way with their waking imagination. Focusing psychotherapist Leslie Ellis worked with survivors of torture who had sought help for their replicative nightmares. After FOD treatment, their nightmares changed: the attacker in the dream changed identity, and the dreamers found that they were able to take action in the dreams in a way they hadn't in the waking-life experience: they could ask for help or stand up for themselves (Ellis, 2016). The dreams also began to weave in other aspects of their waking lives: they became more associative. This study neatly demonstrates how nightmares change in response to treatment as healing begins to take place.

FINAL COMMENTS ON TRAUMATIC NIGHTMARES AND PTSD

Traumatic dreaming is a shared social nightmare. The traumatic dreams that haunt the nights of individuals who have been attacked, abused, displaced, and otherwise traumatised speak to the suffering to which we as a human race expose our fellow humans, and their prevalence sheds an uncomfortable, ugly light on the exercise of power from those who hold it against those who do not. The war nightmares of combat veterans, the sexual molestation nightmares of abuse victims (often women and children), the chase nightmares of refugees forced to flee homes from government and other forces – these collective nightmares tell the stories of the powerless and the vulnerable in human society. Since we share so many nightmares, perhaps it would be helpful for us to actually share them with each other – to make sharing dreams and nightmares a more common practice. We'll look at dream-sharing in the next chapter.

PSYCHOSIS

PSYCHOSIS, SCHIZOPHRENIA, AND SLEEP

'Psychosis', as defined by the British Psychological Society, may involve hallucinations (hearing, seeing, tasting, smelling, or feeling things that others do not perceive), delusions (e.g. paranoia that an organisation is out to get you, or a grandiose belief in yourself such as holding special power or fame if you don't actually have this), disordered thought (confusion, difficulties thinking, difficulties concentrating), and the so-called 'negative symptoms' (such as being inexpressive, withdrawn, listless, or apathetic) (Cooke, 2017). The same symptoms are used to diagnose 'schizophrenia' in the *Diagnostic and Statistical Manual of Mental Disorders*.

For some people, these experiences can be very unpleasant and scary; for others, they are just another way of experiencing reality; and for others still, they may actually be helpful in some way. Naturally, culture plays a large role in how these sorts of experiences are interpreted. In the 'Western' world, people who experience hallucinations, delusions and other psychotic symptoms are often diagnosed with the disorder 'schizophrenia'. This is probably the most well-known disorder that involves psychosis, but other formal psychiatric diagnoses may also include psychosis, such as bipolar disorder and psychotic depression. Hallucination and delusion may also be experienced as a result of various non-psychiatric illnesses, such as Parkinson's Disease.

Sleep deprivation can also cause symptoms very similar to psychosis. Prolonged sleep deprivation is so dangerous that the *Guinness Book of Records* refuses to allow anyone to attempt to break the current record, which is held by Randy Gardner who, in 1964, at the age of 17, without any stimulants, stayed awake for 11 days. On the fourth day he had his first hallucination (thinking that a street sign was a person) and his first delusion (thinking he was a famous football player), and this continued across the following days, along with other symptoms like failing to finish sentences, being paranoid, and difficulty concentrating.

More recently, experimental research has found similar results: if you deprive someone of sleep for long enough, they will begin to exhibit dream-like and psychosis-like 'symptoms' while they are awake. Even one night without sleep will make your thoughts become more disorganised, your perceptions more distorted, and you may even have hallucinatory experiences. It seems as though when we try to stop ourselves from sleeping, the kinds of experiences we have when we sleep seep into our waking world instead. We must have these hallucinatory kinds of dreams, one way or another, even if we aren't sleeping. If you've ever experienced even a fraction of the amount of sleep deprivation Randy did, you may recognise this feeling of drifting into reverie while still awake.

We also know that 80% of individuals diagnosed with schizophrenia have sleep problems (like insomnia or sleep apnoea – when breathing stops and starts during sleep), and treatment with antipsychotics typically increases sleep time and quality. So it's clear that there is a link between schizophrenia and sleep disturbances, although it's not known yet whether sleep disturbances are a symptom or a cause of schizophrenia – or both.

DREAMING AND PSYCHOSIS: TWO SIDES OF ONE COIN?

People have been making associations between dreaming and psychosis for millennia. From ancient Greek to modern philosophers, from psychoanalysts to neuroscientists, dreaming has been seen as 'madness', 'lunacy', 'psychosis', 'delirium', 'schizophrenia', and many other terms that have variously been used to describe similar alternative states of waking consciousness. Just a few examples:

> "There are states, such as madness and dreaming, in which perception is false". – Plato
>
> "The lunatic is a wakeful dreamer". – Immanuel Kant
>
> "A dream is a short-lasting psychosis, and a psychosis is a long-lasting dream". – Arthur Schopenhauer
>
> "Dreaming is not like delirium. It is delirium. Dreaming is not a model of a psychosis. It is psychosis". – Allan Hobson

What is it about dreaming that convinced many pre-eminent thinkers across many different fields to perceive it as a form of psychosis?

SIMILARITIES BETWEEN DREAMING AND PSYCHOSIS

Dreaming and psychosis have many things in common. For one thing, they may both involve hallucination. A hallucination during sleep is called a dream. (However, note that in dreaming, hallucinations are usually visual, whereas in psychosis they are usually aural.) For another, they both often involve delusion. Paranoid delusions and delusions of persecution are common in psychosis – an individual with psychosis may believe that people are out to get them, or following them, or watching them. We also have these kinds of experiences often in dreams: being chased or followed, which we already know is the number one most common dream. Other similarities between dreaming and psychosis include odd uses of speech. The word 'neologism' is used to describe the creation of a new word. It's common in dreams, and it's also common in psychosis.

They are also similar neurobiologically. In both REM sleep (the stage of sleep most associated with hallucinatory dreams) and psychosis, internal perceptions are generated in the brain, emotional centres of the brain are hyper-activated (e.g. the amygdala), the dorsolateral prefrontal cortex (DLPFC) – the part of the brain involved in higher-order executive functions like working memory, organisation, and planning – is relatively deactivated, and there are increased levels of dopamine, a neurotransmitter (a chemical that helps neurons communicate).

DREAMING IN PSYCHOSIS

Individuals with psychosis and/or schizophrenia have many more nightmares than others. In the general population, less than 10% of people have weekly nightmares; in people with psychosis this rises to 70%. This puts those with psychosis on a par with individuals experiencing PTSD in terms of nightmare frequency.

Although dreams of people with psychosis are more unpleasant and nightmarish, research shows that they are no more bizarre than dreams of people without psychosis. On the other hand, people with psychosis have much more bizarre *waking* fantasies than others (Limosani et al., 2011). So although their dreams are no odder than anyone else's, their waking-life thoughts *are*. In other words, people with psychosis experience a more bizarre *waking* reality. This links back to the earlier question of whether dreaming is like psychosis, but it suggests we should switch it around – it's more the case that *psychosis* is like *dreaming*.

This idea is supported by a study by Valdas Noreika and colleagues at the University of Turku in Finland in 2010. They compared the night-dreams and daydreams of people with schizophrenia to those of people without schizophrenia. For those without the disorder, it was very easy to tell which reports were night-dreams and which were daydreams because night-dreams were so much more bizarre. But for people with schizophrenia, the daydreams were so bizarre it was almost impossible to tell them apart from night-dreams. Again, this indicates that people experiencing psychosis are in some respects 'dreaming whilst awake'.

IS THERE METHOD IN THIS MADNESS?

We could conclude, therefore, that dreaming is psychosis. Certainly, this has been the view of some oneirologists, who emphasise the supposedly irrational and nonsensical nature of dreaming. On the other hand, we could instead view the inherently irrational and nonsensical nature of dreaming as merely being a different state of consciousness to linear waking thought. Perhaps dreaming seems like 'madness' simply because we're viewing it with our waking minds. But as a state of consciousness in and of itself, it is perfectly reasonable and has similarities to multiple other states of consciousness.

For example, there has been a long tradition of many famous writers and artists allegedly having experiences like psychosis. Perhaps psychosis and related experiences are intricately interlinked with creativity, just as dreaming and creativity are (as we saw in Chapter 3).

Additionally, just as dreaming and psychosis have often been compared with each other, so have they often been compared to psychedelic consciousness – states of consciousness experienced while under the influence of psychedelic drugs like LSD (acid) and psilocybin (magic mushrooms). All three of these states of consciousness have potential pleasant and enjoyable aspects as well as unpleasant and frightening aspects.[4]

5

DREAM-SHARING

DREAMWORK IN DREAM GROUPS AND PSYCHOTHERAPY

WHAT IS DREAMWORK?

'Dreamwork' comes in two main formal settings: dream groups, in which a group discusses the dreams of its members; and therapy, in which a therapist discusses a patient's dream with them. Others have their own ways of exploring and discussing dreams, such as with a loved one or on internet forums or simply dream journalling alone. There are many different methods of dreamwork. In this chapter, I will discuss some of the most well-known and those that have been most researched by psychologists.

Early forms of dreamwork were Freud's 'free association', and Jung's 'amplification' (see Chapter 2). Modern dreamwork, however, breaks decisively from such psychoanalytical methods. Perhaps the most important distinction between them is that in modern dreamwork there is an emphasis on the authority of the dreamer. In psychoanalytical dream interpretation, the psychoanalyst was the expert and thus had authority over the dream. If the patient disagreed with the analyst's interpretation, this could be dismissed as denial. This removes the dreamer's agency and gives all the power to the analyst. In contrast, a key principle of modern dreamwork is that the dreamer has the final say over their own dream.

DREAMWORK IN THE HERE AND NOW

Nowadays, dreamwork focuses more on exploring rather than interpreting dreams (Ellis, 2019). Dreamwork pioneer Montague Ullman suggested we swap 'dream interpretation' for 'dream appreciation'. Personally, I like the term 'dream exploration' as it gives a feeling for the journey that is often undertaken during dreamwork, and the undefined nature of the destination.

Dream exploration is not intended to uncover the 'true' meaning of the dream – it is impossible ever to know this, since we still know so little about what dreams are, and no single theory of dreaming is agreed upon. Here are a few different ways in which people work with their dreams (see Pesant and Zadra (2004) and Ellis (2019) for more details):

- Making connections between the dream and waking life. Sometimes the connections can be metaphorical.
- Embodying the physical feelings of the dream, getting to its 'felt sense', and using this to go deep into the dream.
- Asking dream group members for their ideas about the dream.
- Engaging with each dream element as a projection of aspects of the self.
- Creating artwork from the dream, either for therapeutic or purely creative purposes.
- Rescripting the dream, especially in order to make nightmares less frightening (see Chapter 4).
- Social dreaming, in which individual dreams are not focused on, but instead collective meaning is found from the whole group's dreams and dream associations.

There are countless other methods besides these, but for the sake of brevity I will focus on methods that have been systematically studied by dream researchers. I encourage anyone interested in dreamwork to experiment with the myriad methods available (see the end of the chapter for some ideas) and to develop their own methods.

DREAMWORK: WHAT IS IT GOOD FOR?

INSIGHT

One of the ideas behind doing dreamwork is that dreams are a potential untapped source of insight: they can show us things about ourselves we might not otherwise know. 'Insight' refers to increased knowledge and awareness about one's self and life and the patterns that are being perpetuated, and the discovery of something new. When uncovering an insight, there is often an *aha!* moment — that feeling you get when something suddenly clicks into place.

INSIGHT FROM DREAMWORK IN THERAPY

Assessing whether dreams are effective in generating insight is difficult to do in a scientific way because even if we can show that someone comes up with new insights after discussing a dream, it may not be the dream that spurred the insight but simply having the opportunity to talk about their life with a therapist.

To overcome this, Clara Hill, at the University of Maryland, USA, designed her experiments to be able to compare the insight her clients gained from dreamwork-based psychotherapy to the amount of insight they gained from doing psychotherapy without working with dreams. Hill developed her own dreamwork method, the 'Cognitive-Experiential Model'. Patients are guided through three stages: the Exploration Stage, in which the dream is told and re-experienced, and waking-life associations are made; the Insight Stage, in which the patient is asked to construct some meaning to the dream; and the Action Stage, in which the patient is asked to change the dream in some way and relate this to changes that they need to make in waking life.

Insight was measured with a questionnaire that Hill and her colleagues created. In all her experiments, dreamwork-based psychotherapy led to more insights than psychotherapy without dreamwork. Dreamwork could be effective even in single sessions. So far so good, then: dreamwork is effective as a therapeutic tool. But what about outside of this context – can dreamwork be beneficial for individuals who don't have a therapist? And what about other types of dreamwork – is it only Hill's method that is effective, or do others work too?

INSIGHT FROM DREAMWORK IN DREAM GROUPS

Addressing these questions are a number of experiments that have been conducted by the Swansea University Sleep Laboratory, headed by Mark Blagrove, and by myself at the University of East London. In a series of experiments, we have used two different dreamwork methods in dream groups to investigate whether they have similar benefits to Clara Hill's method in psychotherapy (Malinowski & Edwards, 2019).

The first dreamwork method used was 'Dream Appreciation', developed by Montague Ullman. This is one of the most widely used methods of dreamwork and is excellent in dream group settings because everyone in the group gets really involved in the session. There are three main stages: (1) the dreamer sharing the dream; (2) the dream group members sharing their own thoughts about the dream; (3) the dreamer responding to these thoughts and discussing the context of their waking life. The group shares their thoughts by beginning with "If this were my dream . . ."; this ensures that they are not telling the dreamer what the dream means, only what it would mean to *them* if they'd had it.

The second method is Michael Schredl's 'Listening to the Dreamer'. I had seen this method in action when I joined in some of Schredl's dream groups and was impressed with how many *aha!* moments there were. In this method, there are four main stages: 1) the group asks the dreamer questions about the dream; 2) the group asks the dreamer to make associations between waking life and the dream; 3) the dreamer identifies patterns in the dream and tries to connect these patterns to waking-life patterns; 4) the dreamer comments on whether they would like to act differently now from what they did in the dream and discusses whether insights from this could be applied to waking life.

In several studies, we found that both Dream Appreciation and Listening to the Dreamer helped dreamers come up with many insights into their own lives. Insight measurements in our experiments were just as high as those in Hill's experiments. Encouragingly, I also found that people who had never done dreamwork before got just as much insight from their sessions as did people who were more experienced. So if you're reading this and are inexperienced but curious, you may take courage from these findings and delve in.

WELL-BEING

Some researchers prefer to focus on well-being rather than insight as an outcome of dreamwork. In another of Clara Hill's experiments, she found that not only insight but also well-being increased. This kind of research is also conducted at the Dream Research Institute (DRI) in London, UK. Nigel Hamilton, Director of the DRI, has created his own dreamwork method: the 'Waking Dream Process'. This method focuses on engaging with the dream through the body. David Billington, a DRI-based psychotherapist who uses this method, found that after using this dreamwork process over a number of weeks, well-being improved among his dream group members. It also helped them come to insights about their own lives and also increased their sense of spirituality.

MENTAL HEALTH TREATMENT

In Chapter 4, we saw that some forms of dreamwork can be incredibly helpful for individuals suffering with excessive nightmares, such as those with PTSD. Image Rehearsal Therapy and Focusing Oriented Dreamwork – both dreamwork methods that aim to change the narrative of scary dreams – have both been shown to be very helpful in this regard.

At the moment, psychotherapists do not, as a matter of course, work with their patients' dreams. Much can be gained from it – especially if the patients themselves are interested in discussing their dreams – but dreamwork does not typically form a part of psychotherapeutic training programmes, and until recently there was scarce information on different methods specifically for those working in these settings. Luckily for the budding psychotherapists out there, there is now (Ellis, 2019).

EMPATHY

So far, we have discussed dream-sharing only in terms of working with our own dreams, for our own insights or well-being – or simply curiosity and enjoyment. But there's more to dream-sharing than this. One group of researchers, led again by Mark Blagrove, has shown that when we listen to someone sharing their dream, our empathy for that person increases. Dream-sharing has been practiced by different societies across the world for thousands of years. Perhaps one of the reasons for this is that it is a form of social bonding, and helps us to get to know, and empathise with, the inner life of those around us. Sharing dreams with others is not necessarily for our own benefit alone but helps us to bond with others, too, and enables others to feel heard.

SOCIAL DREAMING

Dream-sharing, then, is a social experience as well as a personal journey. In another method of dreamwork, Gordon Lawrence's Social Dreaming, the aim of dream-sharing is explicitly interpersonal, rather than personal; it is about the connections between the dreams of different people rather than the meaning of one person's dream. In this method, dream group members share their dreams together, but no single dream is explored in detail. Rather, group members associate from one person's dream to another person's dream and then another person's dream and so on. They can even associate from dreams to things from their waking life if they like. As more and more associations are made, aspects of the dreamers' collective environment coalesce, giving expression to something of their shared realities (political, spiritual, social, and so on).

WHY DOES DREAMWORK WORK?

Just how does doing dreamwork give us insights into ourselves, make us feel better about ourselves, increase empathy, and treat nightmares?

The honest answer is we don't exactly know yet; it works, but *how* is yet to be discovered. In my research, I have found that dreamwork helps people to map from the patterns in their dreams to patterns they keep repeating in waking life, and this was a really helpful source of insight to some people. But my dreamwork method explicitly looks for patterns, so this doesn't tell us much about why other methods work.

Perhaps one of the reasons dreamwork is effective is because dreams unveil uncomfortable, difficult, and often avoided (suppressed) thoughts and memories. As Freud (1900) famously said, dreams may be the "royal road to a knowledge of the unconscious activities of the mind". In Chapter 3, we saw how modern research has supported the idea that dreams picture suppressed material. Could that be one of the reasons why dreamwork is so helpful: it builds a road between our ('conscious') waking mind and our ('unconscious') sleeping mind, laying bare those unpleasant thoughts we've been avoiding?

Another reason why dreamwork is effective could be that it helps us to get in touch with intense emotions. We already know from Chapter 3 that dreams may be working behind the scenes, usually unremembered, to help us process our emotions. Perhaps when we do recall a dream and are able to work through it while awake, this amplifies the emotion-processing work that dreams are already doing.

Dreams often picture the same content over and over again – recurrent dreams, repetitive nightmares, or simply the same theme coming up time and again. When dreams do this, it suggests that something is stuck; it's as if something is repeatedly trying to be resolved but failing. When we work with a dream that has a repetitive theme like this, dreamwork may help this material to become unstuck.

A final thought on this: perhaps dreamwork is partly so powerful because it means working with something that's full of symbolism (see Chapter 3), and, for many people, has a numinous quality (spiritual, mysterious, or simply awe-inspiring) to it. Like working with the Tarot or other occult practices, perhaps dreamwork appeals and is effective because it allows us to get in touch with what Jung called the 'archaic language of parable and myth', which is replete with metaphors and magic. Dreams are an especially powerful tool in this respect since they come from our own minds, so we make up our own metaphors and magic in our dreams.

DO-IT-YOURSELF DREAMWORK

If you want to do your own dreamwork but have no idea how to get started, you could try one of the following simple method on your own (or even start your own dream group); each one is taken from a different dreamwork method. The first thing to do is make sure you're recalling your dreams: you can't get anywhere without any dream recall. You can even work with very short, simple dreams, or single dream images. If you're not recalling many dreams at the moment, try keeping a journal: ask yourself every morning what dreams you can recall, and write anything down, even if it's vague and fleeting. The more you do this, the more you'll recall.

MAKE ASSOCIATIONS TO WAKING LIFE

Once you've written a dream down, go through it carefully and consider each element of the dream – each character, place, object, action, feeling, and so on – and ask yourself whether it has any connection to something from your waking life. Even something this simple can sometimes give you insights into what it was in waking life that inspired the dream. Many dreamwork methods start with or include this stage.

TELL AN ALIEN

In Gayle Delaney's Dream Interview Method, dreamers pretend they are telling the dream to an alien from a planet with no conception of how things are on earth. In this way, dream elements are told in the most basic way, and thus the dreamer learns what *personal* meaning underlies each dream element. Take an example of a cat in a dream – there are many different types of cats, and for each person 'cat' will mean something slightly different. Imagine trying to explain to the alien what a cat is and what the cat in your dream is like – beautiful, independent, hungry, grumpy? This can help to understand what the dream element may be representing.

ASK A FRIEND

In Montague Ullman's Dream Appreciation method, the dream group members say what the dream would mean to them if they had had the dream. They do this by starting, "If this were my dream . . .". In doing this, the group is able to offer their own thoughts without pressuring the dreamer to agree with them. You might like to try a version of this: ask someone in your life what the dream would mean to them, if they'd had the dream, and see if this helps you.

BECOME A DREAM IMAGE

In Gestalt therapy (a type of psychotherapy developed by Fritz Perls), role-play is often used to enable a patient to talk to parts of themselves that they might be hiding from. This can be applied to dreams too. In Bob Hoss's Scripted Role-Play[1] worksheet, you choose an image from your dream that you are drawn to and ask it six questions: what/who are you? What is your purpose or function? What do you like about being who/what you are? What do you dislike about being who/what you are? What do you fear most? What do you desire most? Once all six questions have been answered, imagine it is *you* who is giving these answers, and see if these answers relate to you.

DRAW YOUR DREAM

In some dreamwork methods such as Judy Pascoe's Drawing in the Night, the dream is recreated artistically. Get some plain paper and some coloured pencils and draw your dream: the whole thing, or just one image, or your artistic interpretation of the dream. If you don't like drawing, paint it, sculpt it, make a collage of it, dance it, write a poem out of it, turn it into a story, or use it in any other creative way that you want.

LOOK FOR PATTERNS

In Michael Schredl's Listening to the Dreamer method, dreamers are encouraged to try and find underlying patterns in the dream. Retell your dream in two ways: 1) only telling the actions, such as "I gave someone a present" instead of "I gave my partner a box set of *Game of Thrones*"; 2) only telling the emotions you felt, such as "I was terrified" instead of "monsters were chasing me". This will give you the action pattern and the emotion pattern of the dream. See if these patterns are like any patterns from your waking life, especially ones that you may keep repeating or seem to be stuck in.

CHANGE THE ENDING

In Clara Hill's Cognitive-Experiential Method of dreamwork, the final stage is to consider how the dreamer would like to change the ending of the dream, if they could. Consider whether you would have liked the dream to end differently. Does this relate to changes you would like to make in your waking life?

DREAM THE DREAM ON

In Eugene Gendlin's Focusing Oriented Dreamwork, dreams are viewed as 'unfinished' and dynamic; thus, dreamers are given the option of continuing the dream on from where it ended. If the ending is unsatisfying to you, imagine yourself back into the dream, and see if it can carry on with your waking imagination. There's no need to force it; if it can, it will unfurl naturally before your (inner) eye.

LOOK FOR THEMES

If you start dream journalling, you will end up with a wealth of dreams upon which to draw. When you have done this for a while, you can start looking for themes that repeat in your dreams. Repetitive dream themes are likely to be able to reveal to you issues with which you haven't dealt or that are consistently bothering you.

GIVE YOUR DREAM SOME SPACE

This doesn't form part of any formally developed dreamwork method I know of, but I find that a little space from the dream is sometimes all I need to understand it better: I might wake up one morning having had a dream and be scratching my head in puzzlement about why I had that dream, but when I revisit it a few days or weeks later, its meaning jumps out at me, so self-evident I can't believe I didn't see it before. Don't just discard the dream once you've had it: revisit it days, weeks, months, perhaps even years later, and see if your understanding of it changes.

DEVELOP YOUR OWN METHOD

Once you've tried out a few dreamwork methods and have been journaling for a while, you'll almost certainly start to tweak, refine, and reconfigure these methods and develop your own way of exploring your dreams. You don't have to explore your dreams with insight, well-being, or therapy in mind, if this isn't your interest – these are merely the measurements that have been used in academic research. If you have another interest in dreams that hasn't been discussed here, develop your own method!

A FINAL WORD

Because dreams may reveal things we'd rather not think about, it's important to enter the world of dream exploration knowing you might reveal parts of you to yourself that you might not want to see. Any part of any dream could spur an *aha!* moment – and it won't always be a moment you enjoy. Remember to practice dreamwork safely, with support in place ideally. Maybe join a group with an experienced facilitator if you can. If this isn't possible, try discussing them with loved ones.

6

EXTRAORDINARY DREAMS

LUCID DREAMS, PRECOGNITIVE DREAMS, AND SLEEP PARALYSIS NIGHTMARES

LUCID DREAMS

WHAT IS A LUCID DREAM?

Most of the time when we dream, we have no idea that we're dreaming. Even if something that would be impossible or absurd in waking life happens, we continue along in our dream as if it were perfectly ordinary. However, sometimes, in a flash of insight, we might think, "Wait a minute . . . I'm pretty sure dragons don't exist . . . this must be a dream". Put simply, lucid dreaming is having the awareness that a dream is a dream.

You never have control over a dream as such. You may be able to direct your own actions and influence the dream around you, but you aren't 'controlling' the dream (Waggoner, 2014). Many lucid dreamers find that trying to exert control over a lucid dream may result in them waking up or being unable to do what they're trying to do. And even if you can influence the dream, there's always an element of 'dreaminess' still there: there will always be aspects of the dream that you are not consciously directing.

HISTORY OF THE SCIENTIFIC STUDY OF LUCID DREAMING

Lucid dreaming has been documented and practiced across the world for centuries, both in 'Eastern' traditions (e.g. Tibetan Buddhism;

Norbu, 2002), and in the 'Western' world (e.g. Aristotle; LaBerge, 1988). Despite this, oneirologists took a long time to explore this phenomenon; Freud and Jung, for example, didn't discuss lucid dreams in their theories.

Lucid dreaming became of interest to scientists, however, thanks to some innovative minds in the 1960s–80s. In 1968, Celia Green, who was at the time the director of the Institute for Psychophysical Research in Oxford, UK, published a book called *Lucid Dreams*, which included first-hand accounts from many people who had had lucid dreams – the first of any such English-language publication. In this book, she also pondered how it could be possible to study lucid dreams in the laboratory. She raised the possibility of training participants to somehow be able to communicate with the outside world while they were asleep and having a lucid dream. When a person has a lucid dream, they are aware that they are dreaming, so they can remember what has been going on in the waking world, and they can remember that they are in a psychology experiment, so in theory they could do this. But how? Remember that we're paralysed during REM sleep: we can't move, so it's not as if participants could simply wave a hand or say "Hey, I'm in a lucid dream right now!"

In 1975, English psychologist Keith Hearne figured it out. There's one part of the body that isn't paralysed during REM sleep, and it's the part that REM is named after: the eyes. Hearne's volunteers slept in a laboratory while hooked up to a machine that recorded their eye movements, brainwaves, and muscle movements, and when they had fallen asleep, entered a dream state and became aware that they were dreaming, they signalled with their eyes a prearranged pattern of looking left and then right four times in succession. This signal indicated to Hearne that the sleeping person had now entered a lucid dream while in a REM sleep period, which they could then confirm with their dream report upon awakening. This gave conclusive evidence of the existence of lucid dreams. And once lucid dreaming had been scientifically verified in this way, interest in it among researchers picked up, and lucid dreaming research began to grow in popularity.

WHAT ARE LUCID DREAMS LIKE?

You're having a lucid dream if you know that you are dreaming, and if you manage to remain calm enough to stay in the dream, you may find that you can also direct some of the dream. What do you do when this happens? According to one study, the vast majority of people just want to have a good time. Eighty-two per cent of people studied by Schädlich and Erlacher (2012) said they had used a lucid dream to do something that they considered fun, with flying and having sex the most popular activities. In general, lucid dreams are wonderful to experience – vibrant, colourful, joyful, and awesome. While it is certainly possible to have an unpleasant lucid dream experience, such as being lucid in a nightmare, it's more common to have exciting and pleasant lucid dreams.

WHO HAS LUCID DREAMS?

Some lucky people don't need to train to have lucid dreams; they just have them. But personality seems unrelated to lucid dreaming – at least, this is the case for the 'Big 5' personality traits of neuroticism, open-mindedness, agreeableness, conscientiousness, and extraversion. So who does have spontaneous lucid dreams?

Those who practice mindfulness and meditation have more lucid dreams – this makes sense because they are practicing a kind of lucidity during wakefulness, and they also experience this in sleep. Video gamers, who spend a lot of time during wakefulness immersed in virtual reality, are also likely to have lucid dreams. In children, reading (especially sci-fi and fantasy) is correlated with lucid dreaming. In fact, children tend to be spontaneous lucid dreamers more often than adults. Additionally, creative people often have lucid dreams.

HOW TO HAVE A LUCID DREAM

There are many different methods that have been developed for lucid dream induction, and many of them have either anecdotal or experimental evidence for their efficacy. For example, many people have heard of doing 'reality checks' as a lucid dream practice, which is where you repeatedly 'check' that you are awake and not dreaming. An example of this is reading words: if you look at text in waking life, it remains stable; if you look at text in a dream, it usually scrambles and changes before your eyes.

However, it can often take months of practice for things like reality checks to work, which can be frustrating and cause many people to give up before they succeed. It's also unhelpful for research, because we need to be able to reliably induce a lucid dream in someone when they are sleeping in a lab if we want to study them.

Luckily for us, there are two very effective methods for inducing lucid dreams that science tells us can work the first time. The first is a cognitive technique, Wake Back to Bed (WBTB) combined with the Mnemonic Induction of Lucid Dreams (MILD). The second is a psychoactive substance, galantamine.[1]

WBTB + MILD

A group of experimenters tested out whether a combination of two established techniques might be particularly good at inducing a lucid dream (Stumbrys & Erlacher, 2014). The two methods they combined are the following:

Wake Back to Bed (WBTB): For this part, you need to wake yourself up some time into your night's sleep. The experimenters set the alarm for six hours after the participants went to sleep; others use four and a half hours. (Both four and a half and six hours are divisible by 90 minutes, which is the length of a full sleep cycle.) When you wake up, you stay awake for 30–60 minutes, during which time you should engage your brain with something dream-related, like reading a book about lucid dreaming.

Mnemonic Induction of Lucid Dreams (MILD): This involves bringing to mind the last dream you had, and, with your waking imagination, imagining a moment in that dream at which point you could become lucid. This is usually spotting a moment in the dream when something weird happens, which shows you that you're dreaming. Then, you imagine what you would do while lucid – fly? Have sex? Something else?

These two techniques together are very powerful (i.e. waking yourself up, staying awake for 30–60 minutes, and then when you go back to sleep, practicing MILD). The idea is that you will slip straight into the lucid dream you've been practicing when you fall asleep. The experimenters managed to get a 50% success rate with their participants on the first try. Given how long it usually takes to have a lucid dream for the first time, this was an impressive feat. When I tried their combined method, I had a lucid dream the very first night.

GALANTAMINE

Galantamine derives from the red spider lily (a small red flower native to China, Korea, and Nepal) and the common snowdrop (native to Europe and West Asia). Galantamine has a long history of usage, such as in traditional Chinese medicine. Today, it has been repurposed and is manufactured under the brand names Reminyl and Razadyne, used for dementia patients to help prevent memory loss, improve cognitive functioning, and slow the progression of Alzheimer's Disease. It acts in the brain on the neurotransmitter acetylcholine, which is important for learning and memory and also for REM sleep.

For a long time, galantamine's effect on dreams was only anecdotal. Many people were reporting that it could induce lucid dreaming, but there had been no formal research. Then, just a few years ago, oneirologists confirmed these stories – they produced strong evidence that galantamine was better than a placebo (a capsule made to look like the galantamine capsule but containing no active ingredients) in generating lucid dreams (LaBerge et al., 2018). Furthermore, the effects of galantamine were dose-dependent: the 8mg dose led to lucid dreaming in 42% of participants, whereas 4mg led to lucid dreaming in 27% of participants (and the placebo had the smallest effect, leading to lucid dreaming in 14% of participants).

The evidence for galantamine is strong, and it is easily available to purchase in some countries, such as the USA. However, in other countries it is a restricted substance and can only be obtained with a prescription. There are other options for psychoactive substances that anecdotally are said to enhance dreaming. Huperzine A, an alkaloid derived from the toothed clubmoss plant, which is used in traditional Chinese medicine, acts on the same neural pathways as galantamine. It may produce similar effects, is touted on many lucid dreaming websites as a rival to galantamine, and is readily available to buy. *Calea ternifolia*, also known as bitter-grass, is a plant native to Mexico and Central America used to encourage divinatory dreams. There's also mugwort, which is easy to buy online, and you can even pick it yourself: it tends to grow by water and in wastelands and is easily recognisable by its silvery underside and the smell it gives off if you rub it. Mugwort has been used to promote healing dreams by the Chumash people in North America for centuries. There are no controlled experiments with these substances yet, but we may be encouraged by their long history of usage and anecdotal evidence since this was the case for galantamine. (All of these substance possibilities – and any others you may come across – come with an obvious warning to tread carefully, particularly if you have allergies, health conditions, or are pregnant.)

HOW DO LUCID DREAMS AFFECT ME?

Lucid dreams are experienced as 'real' by the body: one study found that people who did squats in a lucid dream experienced an increase in heart rate, just as they would in doing exercise in waking life. (Not a great way to spend a lucid dream but useful for science.) So lucid dreams are real to the person dreaming – not just that they feel subjectively real, but in terms of their bodily responses.

Since we know lucid dreams have real effects on our minds and bodies, we would expect that what we do in our lucid dreams might affect our waking selves. One suggestion is that perhaps we could practice a skill in a lucid dream and then actually get better at it in waking life. And, in fact, this has been found: practicing simple motor skills in a lucid dream makes people better at them in waking life, such as playing darts (Schädlich et al., 2017). This could be applied to any kind of motor skill you could think of, such as playing sports or a musical instrument.

In addition to practicing skills, lucid dreams may facilitate creativity. Take Robert Waggoner's (2014) experience as an example: he was hosting a radio programme on creativity in dreams, and one caller rang up to tell him about how a lucid dream helped him when he got stuck with a novel he was writing: he would become lucid and then communicate with the characters of the novel, and with their help managed to figure out what to do next.

Another potential use for lucid dreams is treating nightmares. Using lucid dreams as a treatment for nightmares has a unique advantage over other methods as it enables direct confrontation with the nightmare *while it's happening*, as opposed to after it has occurred. However, research into the idea of using lucid dreaming to treat nightmares is currently scarce.

EXTRAORDINARY LUCID DREAMING

So far, we have been discussing what has been discovered about lucid dreaming from empirical and formal experimental investigation. We're now going to leave that behind somewhat and look to the *possibilities* of lucid dreaming that have been suggested but not yet researched experimentally.

One possibility is to seek deep, previously unknown, possibly 'higher' states of consciousness; to explore "the unknown and the ineffable" (Hurd & Bulkeley, 2014) and to commune with the "non-visible awareness behind the dream" (Waggoner, 2014). Naturally, these 'higher' levels of lucid dreaming require strong intention and dedicated practice in the same way that reaching deep states of meditation require much practice.

You could train yourself to 'wake up' in dreamless sleep and experience the disembodied nondual lucidity described in the *Upanishads* (ancient Sanskrit texts of spiritual teaching), which is described in Hinduism as "objectless consciousness" or "pure consciousness", in Buddhism as "the Void" (Gillespie, 1992).

For Tibetan Buddhists (as well as Albert Einstein and some consciousness researchers[2]), waking reality is an illusion just as much as dream reality is. Therefore, lucid dreaming can also be a way to 'practice' seeing through the veil of waking reality, just as it helps us to see through dream reality. When we are able to recognise that a dream is an illusion, it may help us to see that what we think of as our waking reality is also an illusion.

A NOTE OF CAUTION

A question I often get asked is, can training yourself to lucid dream actually be *bad* for you? Some oneirologists think it could be (Soffer-Dudek, 2019; Vallat & Ruby, 2019). One of the reasons is that it could reduce sleep quality; and since we know how crucial sleep is to – well, everything – decreasing sleep time and/or quality might not be wise, at least not regularly. However, oneirologist Michael Schredl has addressed this issue and has found that undergoing lucid dream training does not impact on how refreshing sleep feels.

A second reason is that blurring the lines between dreaming and wakefulness may increase confusion about the boundaries between the two. This could be particularly problematic for people at risk of or currently experiencing psychosis since such individuals already have very dream-like waking realities (see Chapter 4). Indeed, one study found that when people spent two months training themselves to lucid dream, their 'schizotypy' – a measurement of schizophrenia-like thoughts – also increased (Avarim & Soffer-Dudek, 2018).

Plus, as I cautioned at the start of this section, lucid dreaming isn't about controlling the dream per se, and many people struggle to gain control over their lucid dreams. This could result in being *aware* that you're dreaming, without having any control over the content – which could be nightmarish and unpleasant.

Caution should also be exercised with all psychoactive substances, such as galantamine, Huperzine A, and mugwort – both in terms of checking the legality of these substances where you live and in terms of being careful with your own health and well-being.

For these reasons, it's a good idea – as I suggested with dream-work – to make sure you are aware of the risks before embarking on lucid dream training and to do so with adequate support around you in case it goes awry.

PRECOGNITIVE DREAMS

HOW DO PSYCHOLOGISTS RESEARCH PRECOGNITIVE DREAMS?

Like accounts of lucid dreaming, stories of dreams that seem to predict the future (which we now call 'precognitive') have a long and rich history and are well known in some religious texts, such as the Bible. In fact, dreams that apparently tell the future go back at least as far as the 15th century BCE Egypt, when the future pharaoh Thutmose IV was said to have been told how he could become ruler of Egypt by a Sphinx in a dream.

When a person feels like they've experienced a precognitive dream, it seems convincing and real. I've spoken to many people who believe they have had such experiences, and I've had an experience myself that I found very uncanny.[3] In fact, many people report having had at least one precognitive dream in their lifetime (60%, according to Schredl, 2009).

As psychologists, it's our job to try and understand why so very many people believe that they have had an experience that should be impossible according to the classical laws of physics, and we can do so from two different perspectives. Using an anomalistic psychology approach, we can assume that such dreams cannot exist and therefore try to find alternative explanations for why people believe in them. Alternatively, using a parapsychology approach, we can forgo assumptions and devise experiments to investigate the existence or non-existence of precognitive dreams, accepting that we may actually find evidence in favour.

THE PARAPSYCHOLOGY APPROACH

The first psychological experiments with precognitive dreams came at a time when consciousness-expansion was a hot topic both for researchers and the general public: the 1960s. Three oneirologists made history in this decade for their pioneering work with precognitive and telepathic dreams: Stanley Krippner, Charles Honorton, and Montague Ullman. The experiments were conducted at the Maimonides Medical Research in New York; hence, these studies became known as the Maimonides studies.

They conducted two experiments on precognitive dreams with a man named Malcolm Bessant, who was supposed to be particularly gifted with future-telling dreams. Bessant slept in their sleep laboratory and was woken up during the night to record his dreams. The following day, a target word was selected at random by a researcher, which was represented by an image, and a multisensory experience based on this word was designed for Bessant to experience the following day. The person who made the random selection of the word did not know anything about the dreams Bessant had just had. The idea was that if Bessant was truly able to dream precognitively, the dreams he had the previous night should closely match the image that was randomly selected the next day.

For example, on one night, Bessant dreamt of a large building with doctors and medical people from which a patient was escaping. In the morning the word that was randomly selected by someone who had no access to Bessant's dreams was 'corridor', and the image that represented this was *Hospital Corridor at St. Remy* by Van Gogh, which depicts a person in the corridor of a psychiatric hospital. The multisensory experience that was created for Bessant involved him 'simulating' a patient at a psychiatric hospital and walking through a corridor of the hospital. Thus, Bessant had dreamt of a scene that closely resembled the image that was randomly chosen the following day.

Once the procedure had been repeated eight times, three outside judges – who were not present for any of the experiment until now – were given the transcripts from the eight nights of dream collection, and the eight target words that were randomly chosen on each day. Their job was to try and match up the dream with the target word. If Bessant had not been dreaming precognitively, there was only a one in eight chance that a judge would match a dream to the correct target. Conversely, five of the eight dreams were correctly matched to the target words. In other words, Bessant did appear to be dreaming precognitively.

Various subsequent reviews of the data collected from these experiments find convincing statistical effects, both demonstrating the unlikeliness that the effects occurred by chance and also that the effects were pretty big. However, a cornerstone of scientific research is replication: if we want to be sure of a result, especially one as important as the Maimonides studies, we need other researchers to replicate the experiments and get the same results. Unfortunately, many of the experiments that tried to replicate the Maimonides findings failed to do so.

However, these post-Maimonides studies changed many aspects of the original research methodology, which means they were not exact replications. For example, the Maimonides studies were conducted in a laboratory and 'gifted' participants were recruited, and they used stimuli that were likely to elicit an emotional response. Conversely, later studies often did not use laboratories, did not seek gifted participants, and used mundane stimuli.

Because of the many differences in the methods and results of these experiments, it's not really possible to evaluate whether precognitive dreams exist or not yet: some experiments find evidence for it, and others don't. Until we have a large number of experiments that use the same methods, we really can't say for sure one way or the other.

On the other hand, there's actually rather a lot of evidence for predicting future events *outside* of dreams (Mossbridge & Radin, 2018). For example, under controlled laboratory conditions, participants' heart rate and other physiological measurements increase *before* they are presented with an emotionally arousing stimulus but not before they are presented with a calm, neutral stimulus. This indicates that at a physiological level they are accurately predicting what they're about to experience.[4]

THE ANOMALISTIC PSYCHOLOGY APPROACH

If well-designed experiments consistently fail to produce evidence for precognitive dreams, though, how will we then account for the widespread belief in them?

One explanation is that experiences of precognitive dreaming could be a form of déjà-vu (Fukuda, 2002). This suggests that the dream didn't really predict the future, but the future experience generated a feeling of familiarity that is ascribed *back* to the dream. 'Déjà-vu' means 'already seen'; when it is specific to a dream, it's sometimes called 'déjà-rêvé': 'already dreamt'. Given the fact that, over our lifetimes, we will have thousands upon thousands of experiences in waking hours, and thousands upon thousands of dreams at night, there can be little surprise that sometimes they will overlap purely by chance. The feeling of familiarity that comes from déjà-rêvé experiences may feel uncanny but could simply be a chance correspondence between two of many thousands of waking events and dreams.

Even when the recalled dream seems *extremely* similar in one's memory to the waking event, this could be because of how malleable our memories are. Our brains are not computers: we don't file away our memories and then take them back out exactly as we put them in. They degrade over time; they change as we have new experiences; we can even 'remember' things that didn't happen. Apparently precognitive dreams, then, could be explained by the combination of the chance overlap between some dreams and waking events, coupled with the mind's ability to misremember.

This idea is supported by an experiment led by parapsychologist Caroline Watt and her colleagues in 2014 at the University of Edinburgh, UK. Her participants were given some news articles and some dreams taken from a website that hosts lots of people's dreams. The news articles had no direct connection to the dreams, but the participants did not know this and were asked to make as many connections between pairs of articles and dreams as they could in three minutes. Watt found that the more connections participants found to these unconnected article-dream pairs, the more likely they were also to believe in precognitive dreams. This showed that people who believe in precognitive dreaming are also likely to find lots of connections between unconnected things – which supports the idea that precognitive dream believers mistakenly connect dreams they've had with unrelated events in waking life.

Precognitive dream believers are also more likely to experience very vivid and unusual experiences like hallucinations or visitations and are also more likely to value creativity and be more imaginative. Believers, then, seem to be a more imaginative bunch. But does this mean that highly imaginative people are more likely to imagine (perhaps wrongly) that they have precognitive dreams, or are imaginative people actually more likely to *have* precognitive dreams?

We don't necessarily have to choose between accepting the existence of precognitive dreams on the one hand and stating that all believers are deluded on the other. It is also possible that precognitive dreams do exist on occasion *and* that some people see precognition where there is none. Hopefully, future researchers will use the existing research into precognitive dreams and precognition more generally to develop careful, well-controlled experiments. Given how extraordinary the implications would be if experimentation does find clear evidence for precognitive dreams, it's really something that needs to be investigated. But, for now, the answer to the question of whether future-telling dreams really do exist is: only the future will tell.

SLEEP PARALYSIS: THE ORIGINAL 'NIGHT-MARE'

The incubus and the succubus. Ghosts. Witches and hags. Demons and jinns. Alien abductions. That unspeakable evil presence at the end of your bed. What do these magical creatures all have in common?

They may all come (in part at least) from sleep paralysis: the original 'night-mare'.

So what is sleep paralysis, and what is a sleep paralysis nightmare?

In English we get the word 'nightmare' from sleep paralysis: the Old English word 'mare' referred to the succubus or other evil being who came in the night and tried to suffocate the helpless, paralysed sleeper. Nowadays, of course, 'nightmare' has a more general meaning, but originally it referred specifically to sleep paralysis.

Sleep paralysis occurs when a person sleeping suddenly wakes up in their bed and finds that they can't move a muscle. Their eyes are open, they can look around their bedroom, but they can't move. As if that weren't scary enough, sleep paralysis is very often (about three-quarters of the time) also accompanied by an intense feeling of fear and hallucinations of a usually ill-meaning entity, one that may be recognisable from folklore or be in some way spiritual, mythological, or otherworldly. The entity often means the sleeper harm and may approach the paralysed sleeper and attempt to block their breathing by pressing or sitting on their chest. Sometimes, as in the case of the incubus or succubus, the terrifying encounter may take on a sexual nature. In other cases, strange bodily experiences may occur, like the sensation of floating or an out-of-body experience.

It sounds like something out of a horror movie, but sleep paralysis hallucinations are actually very common and occur all over the world. According to some surveys, up to 50% of the population may experience sleep paralysis at some point in their lives.

We don't know for sure exactly what causes sleep paralysis in the people who experience it, but we have identified lots of risk factors – things that make an episode of sleep paralysis more likely. These include having a variable sleep schedule; sleeping on your back rather than your side or front; consuming alcohol before bed or caffeine late in the day; anxiety and depression; stress and trauma, especially post-traumatic stress disorder (PTSD); being overly tired or sleep deprived; and having jet lag. However, you may have experienced all of these risk factors and still never have had a sleep paralysis experience, so how can we account for that?

It may simply come down to individual differences in sleep based on your genetic make-up. Just as genes determine that one person is a nightowl and another is a morning lark, so too may they determine who is susceptible to sleep paralysis and who isn't. So perhaps it's only those with a genetic susceptibility to it that experience it, but the experience occurs more frequently in those individuals when they are also experiencing any of the risk factors previously mentioned. Studies conducted with twins indicate this is likely to be true; identical twins, who share all of their genes, have a much higher concordance rate of sleep paralysis than non-identical twins, who only share about half their genes.

A GLOBAL NIGHT-MARE

Sleep paralysis can strike an unsuspecting sleeper anywhere in the world. But the way in which it is experienced seems to depend in large part on the culture in which the sleeper was raised. The extraordinary similarities between sleep paralysis experiences across the world show that this is a truly universal experience rather than one that has grown from cultural or traditional beliefs in different places; however, the experience is shaped by the belief system the sleeper inhabits.

Let's be globe-trotters for a moment and roam around the world, peering into some of the specific ways in which sleep paralysis hallucinations may manifest in different cultures globally.

ALIEN ABDUCTIONS

Alien abduction experiences have been reported by people in many places, such as the USA, and there's a strong possibility that at least some of these experiences can be explained by sleep paralysis. The victim very often starts out in bed, paralysed; they may be transported to a ship (there's that out-of-body sensation) and may be forced to procreate with the aliens (the sometimes-unpleasant sexual element of sleep paralysis). Obviously, this is all accompanied by intense feelings of fear.

PANDAFECHE

In a region in Italy, sleep paralysis is known as the *pandafeche* attack, which can come in many forms. Some of these forms are clearly recognisable from traditional European folklore – evil witches, for example, or ghost-like spirits. But they also have a rather unusual manifestation of sleep paralysis in this region – a huge, black, terrifying humanoid cat!

GHOST OPPRESSION

Possibly my favourite term of all of the different names given to sleep paralysis comes from China. 'Ghost oppression' features fear, paralysis, a sense of weight on the chest, difficulty breathing, and, as the name suggests, manifests as a ghost.

SE ME SUBIÓ EL MUERTO

In one of the more gruesome accounts of sleep paralysis, Mexico's *se me subió el muerto* translates to "a dead body climbed on top of me", and appears to be describing a sleep paralysis experience: it involves paralysis, chest pressure, a sense of presence, and hallucinations – in this case of a dead body – all hallmarks of sleep paralysis.

THE OLD HAG

In Newfoundland, Canada, the 'Old Hag' or *ag rog* appears as a witch dressed in white. To be 'hagged' meant to awaken in bed at night to find the witch pressing down on one's chest. We get the word 'haggard' from this entity: to be 'hag rid' means to have been ridden by the hag, and over time the word evolved into its current form.

KHMAOCH SÂNGKÂT

In Cambodia, sleep paralysis is known as khmaoch sângkât, "the ghost pushes you down". It refers to a common experience in which an evil entity in the room will sit on, suffocate, strangle, or push down on the sleeper's body, restricting their breathing.

THE JINN

In Egypt, sleep paralysis is experienced as a jinn by many: a spirit entity that originates in Islamic culture, which holds down and strangles a paralysed sleeper and is believed to have the ability to possess and even kill its victims.

POPOBAWA

Zanzibar's popobawa literally translates to 'bat-wing' and is named after the dark shadow that the nocturnal spirit casts upon the wall when it attacks its helpless, immobilised victim.

ALPDRUCK

In German folklore, the Alp is an elven creature akin to the incubus, and the name for 'nightmare' in German, alpdruck, translates literally to 'elf-pressure' or 'elf-oppression', referring again to the suffocating feeling so often experienced during sleep paralysis.

KANASHIBARI

The Japanese word kanashibari translates to "bound in metal", again referring to the sense of immobilisation that defines sleep paralysis.

These are just a handful of sleep paralysis experiences from across the world, but many, many others have been documented too: the *matröd* of Iceland; the *karabasan* of Turkey; the *uqumangirniq* of the Inuit of Alaska, Canada, and Greenland; the *borotat* of Morocco; the *sebeteledi* of Botswana, and so on.

Sleep paralysis even contributed to witch trials. "Spectral evidence" (Adler, 2011) was admissible in many trials, including the Salem witch trials. Transcripts of the trials show that experiences we now recognise as sleep paralysis nightmares were given as evidence against women on trial. For example, against the alleged Salem witch, Bridget Bishop, accuser Richard Coman testified that she had "oppressed him so, that he could neither stir himself, nor wake anyone else, and that he was the night after, molested again in the like manner" (Davies, 2003).

In fact, we can trace the history of sleep paralysis back as far as the ancient Assyrian demon *alu*, which attacked people during their sleep, and the ancient Sumerian demon *Lillu*, forerunner of Lillith of the Talmud. The Ancient Greeks had *ephialtes*, Anglo-Saxons and Old Norse mythology had the *Mara* or *Mare*, and early Christian traditions introduced the incubus and succubus. Clearly, sleep paralysis has occurred throughout the ages and across the world.

WHY IS THIS HAPPENING TO ME?

Given the ubiquity of sleep paralysis experiences in every corner of the globe, it begs the question: why does this happen? According to Adler (2011), although culture plays a big role in determining the nature of the nightmare, and the importance it's accorded, culture does not actually *create* the experience but only shapes it.

Many explanations have been put forth to try to explain what sleep paralysis is, ranging from physical or mental illness to repressed sexual desires (in the psychoanalytical tradition – see also Chapter 2) to religious or paranormal explanations. Another way to approach this question is through the lens of sleep science and oneirology.

Cast your mind back to Chapter 1, when we looked at some of the changes our brains and bodies go through when we enter REM sleep – the stage of sleep most closely associated with vivid, emotional, hallucinatory dreams. Recall that in REM sleep, we experience 'muscle atonia' (i.e. the loss of muscle tone or muscular paralysis). This is totally standard for REM sleep and necessary so that we don't wind up acting out our dreams. Other typical physiological aspects of REM sleep include vivid hallucinations (dreams), shallow breathing (hypoxia), heightened activation of the fear centre of our brain (the amygdala), excitation of the genitals (penile erection or clitoral engorgement), and a heightened threat-detection response. In addition, if we lay upon our back during sleep, muscles in our tongue and oesophagus relax, which restricts breathing and may create a sensation of being unable to breathe.

None of this is unusual, strange, or irregular in REM sleep, but what is irregular is that we aren't supposed to suddenly wake up in our bed with all of these REM sleep physiological changes still occurring. But for some people, for various reasons, these aspects of REM sleep may intrude into wakefulness, and these physiological changes that we go through in REM sleep match up closely to the sleep paralysis experience. Muscle atonia accounts for the paralysis; hypoxia, and the effect on breathing of sleeping on your back, account for the feeling of suffocation or chest pressure; activation of the amygdala accounts for fear; excitation of the genitals accounts for the occasionally sexual nature of sleep paralysis; an active threat-detection system accounts for the harm that the entity often means.

In addition to all of this, it's not particularly surprising, given what we know about how bodily sensations affect dreaming, that the hallucination creates an external agent who is responsible for the suffocation. I remember awakening from a dream once in which someone had just shot me in the stomach, and realised that I did actually have a terrible stomach cramp in waking life: my dream had given the cause of this pain to an ill-meaning dream character. Likewise, in sleep paralysis nightmares, the cause of the chest oppression, suffocation, and fear is projected onto an ill-meaning entity.

EXPLAINING THE ENTITY

Looking for physiological explanations of sleep paralysis, then, yields plenty of hits. But one thing this approach to understanding sleep paralysis doesn't seem able to account for is why the experience often takes on such a distinctively paranormal, folkloric, demonic, or otherwise unearthly form. Although the attacker can be a human intruder, many people experience sleep paralysis as unearthly, even when they themselves do not necessarily subscribe to such beliefs. At the moment, there is no clear explanation for this. Adler (2011) points out that even though we can come up with these biological explanations of sleep paralysis, it still *feels* 'numinous': it still retains that spiritual or otherworldly quality.

Because of this, explaining sleep paralysis with REM sleep physiology may feel incomplete to those who have experienced it. We may be able to explain the paralysis, the fear, the breathlessness, and so forth, but we still can't explain the numinosity. Those intruders – the ghosts, demons, witches, and aliens – feel so intensely *real*, and we don't really have a good explanation for their visits yet.[5]

HOW DO I STOP SLEEP PARALYSIS?

Considering how unpleasant sleep paralysis can be, it's unsurprising that the question on many sufferers' lips is: how do I stop myself from having these experiences?

To some extent, the answer might be that prevention is better than cure since there is currently very little scientific research that's been conducted into treatments for sleep paralysis. However, we know quite a lot about risk factors, so one way to avoid sleep paralysis is to reduce the risk factors as much as possible. That means maintaining a regular sleep schedule, avoiding caffeine and alcohol close to bedtime, using tools to reduce stress and anxiety before sleep, and so forth. Some inventive individuals have even gone so far as to stuff a tennis ball in the back of their pyjamas to try and prevent their sleeping selves from rolling onto their back.

None of this helps if you are actually in a sleep paralysis episode, however, so what to do when you find yourself immobilised with an evil presence approaching your bed? Many people I've spoken to tell me the most sure-fire way to get yourself out of there is to try and move a part of your body – say, one finger – and to concentrate all your efforts on that. Once you've got movement in that finger, you can remove yourself from the whole episode.

Or, you could train yourself to lucid dream. If you can 'wake up' in your sleep paralysis nightmare, you could potentially change the evil entity to something a little friendlier. Ryan Hurd, author of the website www.dreamstudies.org, talks about just this in his article "3 Techniques for Transforming Sleep Paralysis into a Lucid Dream" – and his website is a great repository for much more information about sleep paralysis.

IS SLEEP PARALYSIS ALWAYS TERRIFYING?

No. But it usually is. Exceptions to the typical scary type of sleep paralysis experience are ones in which there is no hallucination; ones in which the floating or out-of-body experience is a pleasant sensation; and ones in which the entity is benevolent rather than malevolent. The latter are relatively rare, but it does happen. If you decide to train yourself to lucid dream to help treat your sleep paralysis, you could turn your terrifying hag into a healing witch (or your evil ghost into a friendly ghost, or your malevolent demon into a benevolent fairy – or whatever is relevant for your particular entity).

Likewise, just as an attack by a malevolent being in sleep paralysis could instead be a pleasant visit from a benevolent being, so can sexual attacks by incubi or succubi, or unpleasant sexual probes by aliens, instead be pleasurable, erotic visits from ghosts, spirits, or other unearthly creatures. Some people recount enjoyable orgasmic experiences with their paranormal visitors in the liminal spaces between wakefulness and sleep.

7

SCI-FI DREAMING

DREAM-HACKING AND ANDROID DREAMS

Sci-fi has had a lot to say about dreaming over the years: film director Christopher Nolan (*Inception*), fiction writer Ursula Le Guin (*The Lathe of Heaven*), anime director Satoshi Kon (*Paprika*), and many others have explored the weird and wonderful world of dreams. In sci-fi, dreams often stop being something that we experience individually, alone, and become something that can be hacked, altered, shared, or even used to wield destruction on the world.

The terrifying/exciting thing is, this is not as far away from reality as you may think. Let's take Nolan's *Inception* as an example. (Warning: spoilers ahead.)

Inception begins with the premise that it's possible to enter someone's dream and extract information from their mind. But Dominick Cobb, played by Leonardo DiCaprio, has been hired to do a more difficult job: rather than extract information, he's been hired to *incept* an idea in a dream, to plant an idea that the dreamer will wake from and think was their own idea.

The film uses many concepts that already exist in dream science. The use of 'totems' to figure out that they're dreaming is a well-known method of inducing lucid dreaming called 'reality checks', as we saw in Chapter 6, for example. Or the concept that we can wake from a dream with a new idea, which is a well-known functional theory of dreams, and there are many anecdotal examples of this, as we saw in Chapter 3. The *Inception* team clearly did their homework.

But what about the parts of the film that are not possible yet? Being able to *see* someone else's dream; being able to *be* in someone else's dream; being able to *remove* material from someone else's dream; or being able to *implant* material into someone else's dream. If all of those things were achievable, *Inception*, and therefore dream-hacking, may be possible. None of these are currently possible, but just how close are we? Do we need to worry about this happening within our lifetimes, or is it something that our grandchildren's grandchildren still needn't lose sleep over?

SEEING SOMEONE ELSE'S DREAMS

We're some way away yet from being able to see someone else's dream on a computer screen, like watching a film, but the journey towards this being possible has started. This particular journey begins in the ATR Computational Neuroscience Laboratories in Japan.

In the first experiment of its kind, a research team led by Yukiyasu Kamitani was able to translate images from the brains of people who were dreaming to pictures of their dreams on a screen (Miyawaki et al., 2012). Volunteers slept in the lab while their brains were being scanned, and upon awakening, were asked to say what they were dreaming of. Later, while awake, they were shown pictures of different types of things we might dream about, like a human face, also while they were having their brains scanned. This way, the researchers knew what neural signature – what pattern of brain activity – to look for when the person was having a particular dream during sleep, and seeing a particular type of image while awake.

In this way, the researchers thought it should be possible to predict what the volunteers were dreaming by comparing their brain activity from when they were dreaming to the brain activity from when they were awake and looking at certain pictures. Brain activity when *looking* at an image of a human face should, for example, be very similar to brain activity when *dreaming* of a human face. So they took all the data they had – the patterns of activity from the dreaming brain and the patterns of activity from the brain looking at pictures while awake – and fed all of it into a decoder. By comparing the two, the machine was able to predict what the images were in the dream with 75–80% accuracy. Pretty impressive!

Of course, this is still a long way from being able to watch a dream on screen, but these are the sorts of developments that need to happen for that eventually to be possible. Kamitani and his colleagues have also been working on scanning waking brains to see if they can map from thought to screen. And at the time of writing, they're getting close.

Take an experiment from 2019 as an example (Shen et al., 2019). In this, volunteers spent their time looking at various pictures, but dreams were not involved this time. While they looked at the pictures, their brains were being scanned by machinery, again designed to record their neural activity. Then, using these brain scans, the experimenters used a computer programme to try to reconstruct, on screen, the images the volunteers had been looking at. The accuracy with which the images were reconstructed on screen was really quite extraordinary.

MANIPULATING DREAM CONTENT

Okay, being able to see another person's dreams might be possible then. Next, let's look at whether we can manipulate what someone dreams of, since there's a decent amount of research into this already, before we go into the murkier territory of entering someone's dream.

TACTILE STIMULATION DURING SLEEP

Altering dream content is something researchers have been trying to do for decades. When they try to do this by exposing participants to stimuli before sleep, it's generally not very successful. But when they try to do this by stimulating participants in some way during sleep, then dream content does often change. You may have had this experience yourself – if you are in discomfort or pain while you sleep, the sensation can become part of the dream, like the example I gave earlier of dreaming of being shot in the stomach when sleeping with stomach cramps. It happens in *Inception*, too, like when the van tumbles over with the inception team asleep in it, and this makes the whole dream-world tumble with it.

Researcher Tore Nielsen at the Hôpital du Sacré-Coeur in Canada wanted to see if this could be recreated in a lab. Before his participants went to sleep, a blood pressure cuff – the type the doctor straps around your upper arm and inflates to test your blood pressure – was affixed around one of their legs. When the participants had entered a REM cycle, the pressure cuff was inflated, slowly enough to avoid waking them up but with enough pressure for it to be clearly felt as a tightening around the leg. Dream reports were collected in the moment just after the pressure cuff was released. Many of the dreams very clearly incorporated the sensation of the tightening cuff: in some, the dreamer simply felt a tightening around the leg in the dream; in others, the sensation was attributed to something completely different: one dreamer had to run through snow, and this made his leg ache; in another, a dream character had a painful leg because a horse had crushed him.

In this way, we have known for some time that dream content can be influenced by stimulating the dreaming body with some kind of sensation. However, this is quite a generic effect: we can get people to dream of having a painful leg, but what use is that if we want to try to control our dream content in more specific ways?

More recently, researchers at the Massachusetts Institute of Technology (MIT) have been developing technology that will allow far more specific content to be implanted into a dream (Horowitz et al., 2018). In Stage 1 sleep, as you may recall from the very beginning of the book, we have dream imagery called 'hypnagogia', and it's this that they wanted to target, extend, and be able to influence. Their invention, which they call Dormio, is worn on the hand like a glove. This glove measures a sleeping person's muscle control. When we transition from Stage 1 sleep to Stage 2, our muscles relax; thus, by wearing the Dormio glove, the researchers could see clearly when their volunteers began to enter Stage 2. When they do, Dormio then speaks to them and tells them that they are falling asleep. This is enough not to wake them entirely but is enough to prevent them from moving into Stage 2 sleep; so they are kept in Stage 1. While this is going on, Dormio can also tell them to think of specific things, like "remember to dream of a rabbit". All six of their participants reported seeing images of the things Dormio told them to dream of.

TARGETED MEMORY REACTIVATION

REACTIVATING MEMORIES DURING SLEEP

Another way of stimulating particular content during sleep is called Targeted Memory Reactivation (TMR). One of the first experiments to use this method was conducted just over a decade ago by Björn Rasch and his colleagues, working at the University of Friborg in Switzerland. Participants watched a computer screen on which images of objects (e.g. a car) were presented in a particular place on the screen, and they had to try to remember where on the screen the object was placed. At the same time as this, the smell of roses was pumped into the room. Then the participants went to sleep, and the smell of roses was pumped out again. Upon awakening, participants' memory for the task was much improved compared to participants who did not smell the roses during sleep. It seemed as if the scent triggered the memory consolidation of that particular experience; it stimulated the brain to rehearse that memory.

TMR has taken off since then. A review of the TMR sleep research by Daphne Schouten and her colleagues at the University of Amsterdam, the Netherlands, concluded that TMR is potentially a very powerful tool for enhancing memory consolidation during sleep. But they also caution that "it should be kept in mind that tampering with evolutionarily conserved consolidation processes . . . is likely to result in undesirable consequences" (Schouten et al., 2017). (Undesirable consequences of new technology? Sounds pretty sci-fi to me.)

But reactivating a memory we already have is still a far cry from 'inception'. For this to be possible, a new memory, or a new thought, needs to be implanted into the mind during sleep. Less research has been conducted to test this possibility, but it has begun. Researchers at the Massachusetts Institute of Technology (MIT) in the USA conducted their experiment with mice (Ramirez et al., 2013). First, the mice spent some time mooching around in one area that we'll call Room 1. During this time, the mice would be learning new memories of Room 1, and neurons in the hippocampus (an area of the brain important for memory) would be activated. The researchers were able to tell which neurons these were because the mice had been engineered to produce a specific protein when they were in a new place.

Then, the mice spent some time mooching around another area, Room 2. In this room, however, they were also given mild electric shocks to their paws. This is a method commonly used to create a fear response. Mice don't like these electric shocks (unsurprisingly), so it activates the fear centres in their brain. When this happened, the researchers also re-activated the neurons that had fired in response to being in Room 1, so that this new fear response was activated at the same time as the memory of Room 1, while they were still in Room 2. Then, when the mice were put back in Room 1, where they had never actually encountered electric shocks, they responded with fear, as if they had. The researchers had managed, then, to implant a fear memory into the mice.

This particular study took place in the waking state, and it hasn't yet been achieved during sleep. Moreover, we don't know what associated dreams would look like during TMR; there's no evidence yet that TMR is accompanied by relevant dream content. However, this kind of research is still in its infancy, and we will be seeing much more of it in future experiments. If and when it is shown to be possible to create new, false memories during sleep, we will be one step closer to inception.

ERASING MEMORIES DURING SLEEP

But TMR isn't just limited to consolidating memories. It can also be used for the exact opposite purpose: erasing memories. In another sci-fi movie, *Eternal Sunshine of the Spotless Mind*, two lovers decide to erase the memories of their former relationship, and this memory erasure takes place during sleep. As the film progresses, the protagonist Joel Barish, played by Jim Carrey, realises that he is sleeping and that his memories are being erased, and changes his mind about having the procedure while it's happening. Still asleep, he tries to stop it, but the memories are erased despite his efforts. This film is over 15 years old now, but the technology it so darkly portrays is being developed now – albeit in a different way.

Sci-fi often depicts horrific unintended consequences of technological innovations, but the innovations themselves are often developed to solve serious real-world issues. In the case of erasing memories, TMR has been developed to help people who have a genuine need to forget – not just because they had a relationship go sour, but because they had a deeply traumatic experience, which may result in PTSD and repetitive nightmares about the trauma (see Chapter 4).

Katharine Simon and her colleagues at the University of Arizona, USA, set themselves the task of discovering whether TMR could be used to encourage forgetting as well as remembering. Their experiment was more complex than the first TMR experiment we encountered earlier. Like the earlier TMR studies, the researchers trained their volunteers to associate an object (e.g. a car) with a spatial location on a computer screen (e.g. bottom left) and also a sound that was related to the object (e.g. car engine revving). Five of these objects were chosen as the experimental objects (we'll call these Objects A), which they wanted to try to induce the volunteers to forget; and five were chosen as control objects to compare against (Objects B).

To try and induce forgetting of Objects A, the researchers next had to train the volunteers to associate forgetting newly acquired memories with a specific sound (a tone, called the 'forget tone'). To do this, volunteers were presented with words (e.g. 'square'), and half of the words were paired with the forget tone. They were instructed that when they heard the forget tone, they should forget the word that was paired with it. In this way, they learnt to associate the forget tone with forgetting.

Next, volunteers went to sleep. During sleep (specifically, slow-wave), the researchers played them the sounds of Objects A along with the forget tone. This was done ten times for each object. For Objects B, no sounds were played. Finally, their memory for the objects was tested a week later. Lo and behold, their memories for Objects A was greatly reduced in comparison to their memories for Objects B; the researchers had successfully induced forgetting with TMR during sleep.

It's not hard to see how this could be incredibly powerful for people with a genuine need to forget, if this research can be applied to more complex memories, like traumatic experiences. However, if and when this technology does exist, no doubt it will also be taken up by commercial enterprises also, who may market it as a way to erase any unwanted memory – *Eternal Sunshine of the Spotless Mind*-style.

DREAM-SHARING

Okay, so we've seen that being able to see a person's dream on a screen may be possible, and implanting and removing memories or ideas may be possible, but what about the final piece of the puzzle: being able to *share* someone's dream?

The final piece is the most puzzling and the one we are furthest away from actually realising. We're now moving from the realms of what is possibly possible into the realms of the maybe-someday-possible based on the current ideas and experiments of some visionary engineers and scientists. We are now talking about being able to share someone else's dream in the moment that they are having it, and experiencing it as if it were your own dream. For this, we need to delve into the world of virtual reality.

Virtual reality (VR) has really taken off recently. Once confined to expensive laboratory equipment, VR machines can now be purchased relatively cheaply for use in your own home. VR has developed so much that it's not just something you see anymore but something that you can feel and even taste. As VR technology progresses, it becomes closer and closer to being like actual reality.

One of these advances is 'shared VR': the experience of being in the same virtual reality as someone else. Rather than video-calling your friends, you would be able enter the same virtual reality as each other and meet each other virtually, in 3D. It's not hard to see how this would be applicable to dreams: once being able to translate dreams to a computer screen has become possible, the next step could be to transpose those images into a virtual reality. Then, another person could access the virtual reality of your dream.

As if that weren't exciting and sci-fi enough, look at what's coming next. The future of virtual reality is 'neuro-reality': brain-machine interfaces (BMIs) in which a VR machine directly interacts with the user's brain (e.g. via an implant or electrodes on the scalp). These machines will allow us to manipulate virtual reality just with our own thoughts. How soon might this happen? By the time you're reading this, it probably already has. Certainly, it is already being developed (Putze et al., 2020).

And this is still only the tip of the iceberg. After this, whole-brain interfaces may be able to communicate via brain signals (thoughts) alone, not just with VR but with other people's brains, as instantly and as effortlessly as the thinking that we currently do. This is in development by a company called Neuralink, founded by Elon Musk. Neuralink wants to build on technological advancements that have already been achieved with BMIs and create a BMI that can be used to both record and stimulate neuronal activity in humans, across a million neurons.

Using this kind of technology, previously unimaginable feats could become reality. One thing that would become possible is direct communication between people's brains. Right now, we're reliant on language (primarily) to communicate. But when whole-brain interfaces become real, one person's brain would be able to interface with another's. In other words, your thoughts would be directly linkable to someone else's thoughts, and your experiences could be experienced by someone else.

For example, let's say you are at home and you're interfacing with your friend who is walking through the woods, when suddenly they notice the smell of honeysuckle in the air. When this happens, specific neuronal patterns of activity in the olfactory bulb of their brain fire. Using their whole-brain interface, which is connected to your whole-brain interface, an analogous pattern of activity in your olfactory bulb is activated, giving you the experience of smelling honeysuckle, too, even though you're sitting in bed with a cup of coffee.

Once we can communicate these kinds of experiences through whole-brain interfaces, it's not too great a leap to communicating your experience of a dream to someone else.

As well as being a cause for excitement, the idea of whole-brain interfaces may also be a cause for concern. Computers can be hacked – not just to steal information from them but also to put information in. Tim Urban, founder of the technology-focused website *Wait But Why*, says: "A clever hacker might be able to change your thoughts or your vote or your identity or make you want to do something terrible you normally wouldn't ever consider. And you wouldn't know it ever happened" (Urban, 2017). Now imagine if that happened to you while you were dreaming. Does that sound a little bit familiar?

We have arrived at *inception*.

DO ANDROIDS DREAM?

In this chapter so far, we've been contemplating how technology may currently, and in the future, allow us to experience dreams differently. Another way in which technology may change the face of dreaming is when technology itself begins to dream. Over 50 years ago, Philip K. Dick asked, *Do Androids Dream of Electric Sheep?* Adapted into Ridley Scott's *Bladerunner* in 1982, Dick's novel explores the humanity of androids and the ethics of the treatment of androids by humans. If and when androids, like the replicants of *Bladerunner*, exist, will they dream? And if they do dream, what will they dream of?

In another sci-fi adaptation, the TV show *Westworld*, this question is explored. In *Westworld*, rich humans can visit a theme park that brings to life different scenes from human history, such as the American

Wild West. Visitors interact with 'hosts': androids who are made to seem as human as possible but who have no will of their own. Hosts' memories are erased every night, ready to start over the next day as if it were their first. But things quickly start to develop; hosts start to have 'reveries' – another name for dreams – which give them access to their old memories. Reveries have been deliberately written into the androids' code by Arnold, one of the founders of the world. This, Arnold had hoped, would eventually lead to the hosts obtaining consciousness.

It's fascinating to me that their route to consciousness is through these reveries. As we have seen in this book, dreams probably do help us to remember, help us to improvise (be creative), and are in our own self-interest to the extent that they are often about us, our lives, our relationships, and our worries. But, of course, this is all still just sci-fi. What does the real world have to say about artificial intelligence dreaming?

Step up, Google DeepDream.

DeepDream is a computer programme created in 2015 by Google engineer Alexander Mordvintsev and his colleagues.[1] They developed a way of training artificial neural nets – systems made of many layers of interconnected artificial neurons, analogous to the neural network of the brain – to recognise and categorise images. To try and understand how exactly the neural net does this, they wanted to understand what kinds of patterns the different layers of the network picked out. For example, one layer of an image could be 'corner' (a simple layer) while another layer could be for specific shapes like 'tree' (a complex layer).

Then, it is possible to have the network enhance an image by having it feed these layers back into itself. For example, if you asked it to emphasise a specific pattern in the image and then repeatedly feed this pattern back into the neural network, an image of one tree would become an image of many trees superimposed on the original image.

Rather beautifully, the creators of this technique call it *inceptionism*!

Following this, they created the DeepDream Generator, which anyone can use by simply uploading an image and running it through the generator. The final image often ends up being very psychedelic: the sort of thing you might see if you'd taken a tab of acid (LSD) or gone on a magic mushroom (psilocybin) trip. Since DeepDream images are similar to acid-induced hallucinations, this might mean that what DeepDream is doing to artificial neural nets and what psychedelics do to human neural nets is also similar: superimposing patterns identified in the visual scene back onto the scene itself. Perception of visual layers in humans is usually an unconscious process, but under the influence of psychedelics, these layers may become superimposed into our conscious visual perception and even fed back repeatedly until we perceive the trippy world of psychedelic hallucination that's part-normal reality and part-visual hallucination.

Although hallucination is different to dreaming, it can be thought of as a form of 'dreaming whilst awake'. One of the long-standing theories about dreaming (from Freud onwards) is that it can reveal unconscious parts of our minds to us (i.e. things that we are not normally aware of). In psychedelic hallucination, perhaps the unconscious process of visual pattern perception is revealed to us through the kind of repeated superimposition of patterns that DeepDream applies to images. And another commonality between psychedelic and dreaming consciousness is that both can make previously suppressed or forgotten emotional material rise to the surface again – again, making something previously unconscious conscious.

So the name alone isn't all DeepDream has in common with human dreaming. DeepDream uses artificial neural networks to create what end up as very psychedelic images. In psychedelic consciousness we may hallucinate – in other words, have a kind of 'waking dream', and there are many other similarities between the two states of consciousness.[2] As DeepDream and similar programmes develop, it will be fascinating to see in what other ways computer 'dreaming' may overlap with human dreaming and what insights these overlaps can tell us.

ANDROID PSYCHOLOGY

Projecting ourselves much, much further into the future, then, we may find that one day androids really do dream. You might be wondering why this is relevant to this book – what have android dreams got to do with *The Psychology of Dreaming*? For one thing, it raises the question of whether androids will be able to dream at all, because this depends on how we define 'dream', which takes us back to the beginning of the book. There, we defined dreaming as 'conscious experiences during sleep'. But will androids sleep, and can they ever be conscious? Of course, these questions are far too weighty for this book, but they are questions future researchers and ethicists will need to address.

Even if you're unconvinced of the relevance of computer dreams for human psychology, they're still relevant for *computers* – and therefore maybe someday for androids. If we do eventually cohabit with androids, will 'Android Psychology' one day become a branch of psychology, alongside other branches like 'Health Psychology' and 'Forensic Psychology'? Books such as Dick's *Do Androids Dream of Electric Sheep?* have been asking questions about the ethics of building androids and how we will treat them for years, and AI innovators will, perhaps, one day need to consider these ethics for real. Maybe one day psychology will join that conversation.

FURTHER READING

Adler, S. R. (2011). *Sleep Paralysis: Night-Mares, Nocebos, and the Mind-Body Connection*. Rutgers University Press.

Artemidorus. (2012). *Oneirocritica* (D. E. Harris-McCoy, Trans.). Oxford: Oxford University Press.

Barrett, D. (1996). *Trauma and Dreams*. Cambridge, MA: Harvard University Press.

Barrett, D. (2001). *The Committee of Sleep: How Artists, Scientists, and Athletes Use Dreams for Creative Problem-Solving — and How You Can Too*. Crown and Random House.

Cartwright, R. (2011). *The Twenty-Four Hour Mind: The Role and Sleep and Dreaming in Our Emotional Lives*. Oxford: Oxford University Press.

Cheung, T., & Mossbridge, J. (2019). *The Premonition Code: The Science of Precognition*. Watkins Publishing.

Domhoff, G. W. (2003). *The Scientific Study of Dreams*. Washington, DC: APA Press.

Ellis, L. A. (2019). *A Clinician's Guide to Dream Therapy: Implementing Simple and Effective Dreamwork*. Routledge.

Freud, S. (1900). *The Interpretation of Dreams*. Hertfordshire, UK: Wordsworth.

Golin, S., & Bregman, A. (Producers), & Gondry, M. (Director). (2004). *Eternal Sunshine of the Spotless Mind*. USA: Focus Features.

Hall, C. S., & Nordby, V. J. (1972). *The Individual and His Dreams*. New American Library.

Hartmann, E. (1998). *Dreams and Nightmares: The Origin and Meaning of Dreams*. Cambridge, MA: Perseus Publishing.

Hartmann, E. (2011). *The Nature and Functions of Dreaming*. Oxford: Oxford University Press.

Hurd, R., & Bulkeley, K. (2014). *Lucid Dreaming: New Perspectives on Consciousness in Sleep*. CA: Praeger.

Jung, C. G. (2002). *Dreams* (R. F. C. Hull, Trans.). London, UK: Routledge.

LaBerge, S. (2009). *A Concise Guide to Awakening in Your Dreams and in Your Life*. Sounds True.

Lakoff, G., & Johnson, M. (2003). *Metaphors We Live By*. University of Chicago Press.

Lawrence, G. (2005). *Introduction to Social Dreaming*. Karnac Books.

Le Guin, U. (2001). *The Lathe of Heaven*. Gateway.

Sacks, O. (2013). *Hallucinations*. Picador.

Sharpless, B. A., & Doghramji, K. (2015). *Sleep Paralysis: Historical, Psychological, and Medical Perspectives*. Oxford University Press.

Smith, C. T. (2014). *Heads-up Dreaming: How Your Dreams Can Predict Your Future and Change Your Life*. San Francisco, CA: Turning Stone Press.

Thomas, E., & Nolan, C. (Producers), & Nolan, C. (Director). (2010). *Inception*. USA: Warner Bros. Pictures.

Ullman, M., & Krippner, S. (1973). *Dream Telepathy: Experiments in Noctural ESP*. Baltimore: Penguin.

Ullman, M., & Zimmerman, N. (1986). *Working with Dreams: Self-Understanding, Problem-Solving, and Enriched Creativity Through Dream Appreciation*. Los Angeles: Jeremy P. Tarcher.

Urban, T. (2017). *Neuralink and the brain's magical future*. Retrieved from https://wait butwhy.com/2017/04/neuralink.html.

Valli, K., & Hoss, R. J. (Eds.). (2019). The neuroscience of dreaming. In *Dreams: Understanding Biology, Psychology, and Culture*, Vol. I, Chapter 2. Santa Barbara, CA: Greenwood.

Walker, M. (2017). *Why We Sleep*. Penguin Random House.

NOTES

INTRODUCTION

1 Of course, we don't recall all of our dreams, but we are all having them. We have about five dreams every night. Some people remember almost all of their dreams, other people remember none, but careful lab-based research (in which volunteers are awoken repeatedly throughout the night) shows us that we all dream – even the people who usually don't remember any of their dreams. The only people who may genuinely have no dreams are those with brain damage to a specific location (see Chapter 2 for details).

CHAPTER 1

1 The word 'conscious' here means that there is a subjective, qualitative feel to the experience.
2 If you would like to know more about other ways to define dreaming, visit https://oneirology.co.uk/defining-dream/.
3 The exception here is for people born without the ability to see. For more on the dreams of blind individuals, see https://oneirology.co.uk/dreams-of-congenitally-blind-individuals/.
4 If you'd like to know more about this, see https://oneirology.co.uk/childrens-dreams/.
5 If you'd like to read some of the evidence that favours the idea of animal dreaming, see https://oneirology.co.uk/animal-dreams/.

6 If you're interested in learning more about how oneirologists analyse dreams, head over to https://oneirology.co.uk/analysing-dream-data/.

CHAPTER 2

1 This section does not include 'The Dreamtime' of Aboriginal Australia because of the uncertainty of how related this is to dreaming; 'The Dreamtime' may be a mistranslation given by early English-speaking anthropologists. For more on this, see https://oneirology.co.uk/the-dreamtime/.

2 The 'dream rebound effect' – for more on this, see https://oneirology.co.uk/the-dream-rebound-effect/, or my article "Was Freud About Dreams Right After All?" (Malinowski, 2016).

3 https://dreams.ucsc.edu/Library/fmid.html

4 Ponto-geniculo-occipital, or PGO, waves are sudden bursts of synchronised neuronal activity which are generated in the pons, then project to the geniculate nucleus in the thalamus, and finally to the occipital cortex. PGO waves are important for REM sleep and also for visual perception.

CHAPTER 3

1 If this idea is of interest to you, see https://oneirology.co.uk/the-no-function-theory-of-dreams/.

2 See https://oneirology.co.uk/the-dream-lag-effect/.

3 See https://oneirology.co.uk/animal-dreams/.

4 In a replication experiment, Wamsley and Stickgold (2019) again found that sleep plus dreaming of the maze was the most beneficial combination, but this time they also found that daydreaming of it was beneficial. In both studies, they also found that participants who did dream of the maze were worse at navigating it at the beginning of the study than those who did not – suggesting that the former had much more to learn than the latter.

5 If you want to know more about ways in which we *do* dream about sex, see https://oneirology.co.uk/sex-dreams/.

CHAPTER 4

1 The 'DSM' – the controversial 'psychiatric bible' which sets out the guidelines for making formal psychiatric diagnoses.

2 *A note on terminology*. In this chapter, I will be using terms used in mental health research and psychiatric diagnostic criteria. As such, you will see terms like

'psychiatric diagnosis', 'disorder', 'symptoms', 'mental health', and so forth. These terms are congruent with the medical approach to mental health. There are many people who would object to these terms, and the medical approach to mental health is something that should be carefully critiqued, especially by students of psychology. However, since these are the terms that are currently favoured in research, these are the terms I will use in this chapter, whilst recognising that they are problematic and likely to fall out of favour in the fullness of time, as the terminology du jour always eventually does.

3 See https://oneirology.co.uk/the-dream-rebound-effect/.

4 If you want to know more about how dreaming and psychedelic experiences are similar, and why I think this similarity is important, see https://oneirology.co.uk/dreaming-and-psychedelic-consciousness/.

CHAPTER 5

1 www.dreamscience.org/wp-content/uploads/2019/03/Scripted-Role-Play-6-magic-questions.pdf

CHAPTER 6

1 Although there are many portable devices that claim to be able to induce lucid dreams, at the time of writing they have not been independently tested for effectiveness.

2 E.g. Anil Seth, Professor of Cognitive and Computational Neuroscience at the University of Sussex, UK, www.youtube.com/watch?v=lyu7v7nWzfo.

3 You can read about this here: https://oneirology.co.uk/precognitive-dreaming-a-personal-account/.

4 Naturally, with a topic as controversial as precognition, there are dissenters; for more discussion of this paper, see *Psychology of Consciousness*, 5(1) for various critiques of this paper and the authors' response to these critiques.

5 If you're interested in my speculative musings on how sleep paralysis may relate to psychedelic consciousness, especially with DMT, see https://oneirology.co.uk/sleep-paralysis-dmt-and-the-entity/.

CHAPTER 7

1 https://ai.googleblog.com/2015/06/inceptionism-going-deeper-into-neural.html

2 See https://oneirology.co.uk/dreaming-and-psychedelic-consciousness/.

REFERENCES

Adler, S. R. (2011). *Sleep Paralysis: Night-Mares, Nocebos, and the Mind-Body Connection*. Rutgers University Press.

Arnulf, I. (2019). Dreaming in parasomnias. In K. Valli & R. J. Hoss (Eds.), *Dreams: Understanding Biology, Psychology, and Culture*, Vol. I. (pp. 238–249). CA: Greenwood.

Arnulf, I., Grosliere, L., Le Corvec, T., Golmard, J.-L., Lascols, O., & Duguet, A. (2014). Will students pass a competitive exam that they failed in their dreams? *Consciousness and Cognition, 29,* 36–47.

Avarim, L., & Soffer-Dudek, N. (2018). Lucid dreaming: Intensity, but not frequency, is inversely related to psychopathology. *Frontiers in Psychology, 9*(384), 1–16.

Baldock, J. (Ed.). (2013). *The Tibetan Book of the Dead*. Arcturus Publishing Ltd.

Barrett, D. (1993). The "committee of sleep": A study of dream incubation for problem solving. *Dreaming, 3*(2), 115–122.

Billington, D. (2014). *So you shall become: Client experience of the waking dream process*. Retrieved from www.driccpe.org.uk/?portfolio-view=1575-2.

Blagrove, M., Hale, S., Lockheart, J., Carr, M., Jones, A., & Valli, K. (2019). Testing the empathy theory of dreaming: The relationships between dream sharing and trait and state empathy. *Frontiers in Psychology, 10,* 1351.

Bulkeley, K. (2004). Dreaming Is Play II: Revonsuo's Threat Simulation Theory in Ludic Context. *Sleep & Hypnosis, 6*(3), 119–129.

Bulkeley, K. (2012, June 22–26). Word searching as a tool of dream content analysis. *International Association for the Study of Dreams Conference*. Berkeley, CA.

Bulkeley, K., & Bulkeley, P. (2005). *Dreaming Beyond Death: A Guide to Pre-death Dreams and Visions*. Boston, MA: Beacon Press.

Cartwright, R. (1992). *Crisis Dreaming: Using Your Dreams to Solve Your Problems*. New York: Harper Collins.

Cooke, A., & British Psychological Society, Division of Clinical Psychology (2017). *Understanding Psychosis and Schizophrenia*.

Davidson, J., & Lynch, S. (2012). Thematic, literal and associative dream imagery following a high-impact event. *Dreaming*, 22(1), 58–69.

Davies, O. (2003). The nightmare experience, sleep paralysis, and witchcraft accusations. *Folklore*, 114(2), 181–203.

De Koninck, J., Christ, G., Hébert, G., & Rinfret, N. (1990, June). Language learning efficiency, dreams and REM sleep. *Psychiatric Journal of the University of Ottawa*, 15(2), 91–92.

De Koninck, J., Christ, G., Rinfret, N., & Proulx, G. (1988, June). Dreams during language learning: When and how is the new language integrated? *Psychiatric Journal of the University of Ottawa*, 13(2), 72–74.

De Koninck, J., Prévost, F., & Lortie-Lussier, M. (1996). Vertical inversion of the visual field and REM sleep mentation. *Journal of Sleep Research*, 5, 16–20. doi:10.1046/j.1365-2869.1996.00001.x.

Delaney, G. (1991). *Breakthrough Dreaming*. New York: Bantam Books.

Domhoff, G. W. (1993). The repetition of dreams and dream elements: A possible clue to a function of dreams? In A. Moffitt, M. Kramer, & R. Hoffmann (Eds.), *The Functions of Dreaming* (pp. 293–320). Albany: SUNY Press.

Domhoff, G. W. (1996). *Finding Meaning in Dreams: A Quantitative Approach*. New York: Plenum Press.

Domhoff, G. W. (2001). A new neurocognitive theory of dreams. *Dreaming*, 11(1), 13–33.

Domhoff, G. W. (2003). *The Scientific Study of Dreams*. Washington, DC: APA Press.

Easwaran, E. (Trans.). (2007). *The Upanishads*. Nilgiri Press.

Ellis, L. A. (2016). Qualitative changes in recurrent PTSD nightmares after focusing-oriented dreamwork. *Dreaming*, 26(3), 185–201.

Fukuda, K. (2002). Most experiences of precognitive dream could be regarded as a subtype of Déjà-vu Experiences. *Sleep and Hypnosis*, 4(3), 111–114.

Garfield, P. (1996). Dreams in bereavement. In D. Barrett (Ed.), *Trauma and Dreams* (pp. 186–211). Cambridge, MA: Harvard University Press.

Gendlin, E. (1986). *Let Your Body Interpret Your Dreams*. Chiron Publications.

Gillespie, G. (1992). Light in lucid dreams: A review. *Dreaming, 2*(3), 167–179.

Green, C. (1968). *Lucid Dreams*. Whitstable: Kent.

Horowitz, A. et al. (2018). *Dormio: Interfacing with dreams. Extended Abstracts of the 2018 CHI Conference on Human Factors in Computing Systems*. New York: ACM.

Hall, C. S. (1953). A cognitive theory of dreams. *The Journal of General Psychology, 48*, 169–186.

Hall, C. S., & van de Castle, R. (1966). *The Content Analysis of Dreams*. New York: Appleton-Century-Crofts.

Harrington, M. O., Pennington, K., & Durrant, S. J. (2017). The "Affect Tagging and Consolidation" (ATaC) model of depression vulnerability. *Neurobiology of Learning and Memory*.

Hearne, K. (1982). Keith Hearne's work on lucid dreaming. *Lucidity Letter, 1*(3), 1–4.

Henrich, J., Heine, S. J., & Norenzayan, A. (2010). The weirdest people in the world? *Behavioral and Brain Sciences, 33*(2–3), 61–83.

Hill, C. (2019). Benefits of dreamwork in psychotherapy. In K Valli, & R. J. Hoss (Eds.), *Dreams: Understanding Biology, Psychology, and Culture*, Vol. 2 (pp. 461–469). Santa Barbara, CA: Greenwood.

Hobson, J. A., & McCarley, R. W. (1977, December). The brain as a dream state generator: An activation-synthesis hypothesis of the dream process. *The American Journal of Psychiatry, 134*(12), 1335–1348.

Hughes, J. D. (2000). Dream interpretation in ancient civilizations. *Dreaming, 10*(1), 7–18.

Hurd, R. (n.d.). *3 techniques for transforming sleep paralysis in to a lucid dream*. Retrieved from http://dreamstudies.org/2011/02/08/3-techniques-for-transforming-sleep-paralysis-into-a-lucid-dream/

Hurd, R., & Bulkeley, K. (Eds.). *Lucid Dreaming: New Perspectives on Consciousness in Sleep*. CA: Praeger.

Jung, C. G. (1934). The practical use of dream analysis. In C. G. Jung (Ed., R. F. C. Hull, Trans.), *Dreams* (pp. 87–108). London, UK: Routledge.

King, J., & Sheehan, J. R. (1996). Identifying sexual trauma histories from patterns of sleep and dreams. In D. Barrett (Ed.), *Trauma and Dreams* (pp. 56–67). Cambridge, MA: Harvard University Press.

Krakow, B., & Zadra, A. (2006). Clinical management of chronic nightmares: Imagery rehearsal therapy. *Behavioral Sleep Medicine*, 4(1), 45–70.

LaBerge, S. (1988). Lucid dreaming in western literature. In J. Gackenbach & S. LaBerge (Eds.), *Conscious Mind, Sleeping Brain: Perspectives on Lucid Dreaming* (pp. 11–26). New York: Springer.

LaBerge, S., LaMarca, K., & Baird, B. (2018). Pre-sleep treatment with galantamine stimulates lucid dreaming: A double-blind, placebo-controlled, crossover study. *PLoS ONE*, 13(8).

Lavie, P., & Kaminer, H. (1991). Dreams that poison sleep: Dreaming in Holocaust survivors. *Dreaming*, 1(1), 11–21.

Limosani, I., D'Agostino, A., Manzone, M. L., & Scarone, S. (2011). Bizarreness in dream reports and waking fantasies of psychotic schizophrenic and manic patients: Empirical evidences and theoretical consequences. *Psychiatry Research*, 189(2), 195–199.

Malinowski, J. E. (2016). Was Freud right about dreams after all? Here's the research that helps explain it. *The Conversation*. Retrieved from https://theconversation.com/was-freud-right-about-dreams-after-all-heres-the-research-that-helps-explain-it-60884.

Malinowski, J. E., & Edwards, C. (2019). Evidence of insight from dreamwork. In K. Valli & R. J. Hoss (Eds.), *Dreams: Understanding Biology, Psychology, and Culture*, Vol. 2 (pp. 469–477). Santa Barbara, CA: Greenwood.

Malinowski, J. E., & Horton, C. L. (2014a). Memory sources of dreams: The incorporation of autobiographical rather than episodic experiences. *Journal of Sleep Research*, 23(4), 441–447.

Malinowski, J. E., & Horton, C. L. (2014b). Evidence for the preferential incorporation of emotional waking-life experiences into dreams. *Dreaming*, 24(1), 18–31.

Malinowski, J. E., & Horton, C. L. (2015). Metaphor and hyperassociativity: The imagination mechanisms behind emotion assimilation in sleep and dreaming. *Frontiers in Psychology*, 6.

Miyawaki, Y., Uchida, H., Yamashita, O, Sato, M., Morito, Y., Tanabe, H. C., Sadato, N., & Kamitani, Y. (2012). Visual image reconstruction from human brain activity using a combination of multiscale local image decoders. *Neuron*, 60(5), 915–929.

Mossbridge, J. A., & Radin, D. (2018). Precognition as a form of prospection: A review of the evidence. *Psychology of Consciousness: Theory, Research, and Practice*, 5(1), 78–93.

Nielsen, T. A., McGregor, D. L., Zadra, A., Ilnicki, D., & Ouellet, L. (1993). Pain in dreams. *Sleep*, 16(5), 490–498.

Norbu, C. N. (2002). *Dream Yoga and the Practice of Natural Light*. New York: Snow Lion.

Noreika, V., Valli, K., Markkula, J., Seppälä, K., & Revonsuo, A. (2010). Dream bizarreness and waking thought in schizophrenia. *Psychiatry Research*, 178(3), 562–564.

Owczarski, W. (2018). Adaptive nightmares of holocaust survivors: The Auschwitz camp in the former inmates' dreams. Dreaming, 28(4), 287–302.

Pascoe, J. M. (2016). *Drawing dreams: The transformational experience of expressing dream imagery as art*. Retrieved from www.driccpe.org.uk/?portfolio-view=drawing-dreams-the-transformational-experience-of-expressing-dream-imagery-as-art.

Peden, A. M. (1985). Macrobius and medieval dream literature. *Medium Aevum*, 54, 59–73.

Pesant, N., & Zadra, A. (2004). Working with dreams in therapy: What do we know and what should we do? *Clinical Psychology Review*, 24(5), 489–512.

Punamäki, R.-L., Ali, K. J., Ismahil, K. H., & Nuutinen, J. (2005). Trauma, dreaming, and psychological distress among Kurdish children. *Dreaming*, 15(3), 178–194.

Putze, F., Vourvopoulos, A., Lécuyer, A., Krusienski, D., Mullen, T., & Herff, C. (2020). Editorial: Brain-Computer interfaces and augmented/virtual reality. *Frontiers in Human Neuroscience*. doi:10.3389/fnhum.2020.00144.

Pynoos, R. S. et al. (1987). Life threat and posttraumatic stress in school-age children. *Archives of General Psychiatry*, 44(12), 1057.

Quartini, A., Anastasia, A., Bersani, F. S., Melcore, C., Albano, G., Colletti, C., Valeriani, G., & Bersani, G. (2014). Changes in dream experience in relation with antidepressant escitalopram treatment in depressed female patients: A preliminary study. *Riv Psichiatr*, 49(4), 187–191.

Ramirez, S., Liu, X., Lin, P.-A., Suh, J., Pignatelli, M., Redondo, R. L., Ryan, T. J., & Tonegawa, S. (2013). Creating a false memory in the Hippocampus. *Science*, 341(6144), 387–391.

Rasch, B., Buchel, C., Gais, S., & Born, J. (2007). Odor cues during slow-wave sleep prompt declarative memory consolidation. *Science*, 315(5817), 1426–1429.

Raskind, M. A., Peskind, E. R., Chow, B., Harris, C., Davis-Karim, A., Holmes, H. A., Hart, K. L., McFall, M., Mellman, T. A., Reist, C., Romesser, J., Rosenheck, R., Shih, M.-C., Stein, M. B., Swift, R., Gleason, T., Lu, Y., & Huang, G. D.

(2018). Trial of prazosin for post-traumatic stress disorder in military veterans. *New England Journal of Medicine*, 378(6), 507–517.

Revonsuo, A. (2000). The reinterpretation of dreams: An evolutionary hypothesis of the function of dreaming. *Behavioral and Brain Sciences*, 64.

Revonsuo, A., Tuominen, J., & Valli, K. (2015). The avatars in the machine: Dreaming as a simulation of social reality. In T. Metzinger & J. M. Windt (Eds.), *Open MIND: 32(T)*. Frankfurt am Main: MIND Group.

Schädlich, M., & Erlacher, D. (2012). Applications of lucid dreams: An online study. *International Journal of Dream Research*, 5(2), 134–138.

Schädlich, M., Erlacher, D., & Schredl, M. (2017). Improvement of darts performance following lucid dream practice depends on the number of distractions while rehearsing within the dream – a sleep laboratory pilot study. *Journal of Sports Sciences*, 35(23), 2365–2372.

Schouten, D. I., Pereira, S. I. R., Tops, M., & Louzada, F. M. (2017). State of the art on targeted memory reactivation: Sleep your way to enhanced cognition. *Sleep Medicine Reviews*, 32, 123–131.

Schredl, M. (2008). Laboratory references in dreams: Methodological problem and/or evidence for the continuity hypothesis of dreaming? *International Journal of Dream Research*, 1(1), 3–6.

Schredl, M. (2009). Frequency of precognitive dreams: Association with dream recall and personality variables. *Journal of the Society for Psychical Research*, 73(2), 895.

Schredl, M. (2015). The continuity between waking and dreaming: Empirical research and clinical implications. In M. Kramer & M. Glucksman (Eds.), *Dream Research – Contributions to Clinical Practice* (pp. 27–37). New York: Routledge.

Schredl, M., Dyck, S., & Khnel, A. (2020). Lucid dreaming and the feeling of being refreshed in the morning: A diary study. *Clocks & Sleep*, 2, 54–60.

Schreuder, B. J. N., van Egmond, M., Kleijn, W. C., & Visser, A. T. (1998). Daily reports of posttraumatic nightmares and anxiety dreams in Dutch war victims. *Journal of Anxiety Disorders*, 12(6), 511–524.

Shen, G., Horikawa, T., Majima, K., & Kamitani, Y. (2019). Deep image reconstruction from human brain activity. *PLOS Computational Biology*, 15(1), e1006633.

Siclari, F., Baird, B., Perogamvros, L., Bernardi, G., LaRocque, J. J., Riedner, B., Boly, M., Postle, B. R., & Tononi, G. (2017). The neural correlates of dreaming. *Nature Neuroscience*, 20(6), 872–878.

Sierra-Siegert, M., Jay, E., Florez, C., & Garcia, A. E. (2019). Minding the dreamer within: An experimental study on the effects of enhanced dream recall on creative thinking. *The Journal of Creative Behavior*, 53(1), 83–96.

Simon, K. C. N. S., Gómez, R. L., & Nadel, L. (2018). Losing memories during sleep after targeted memory reactivation. *Neurobiology of Learning and Memory*, 151, 10–17.

Soffer-Dudek, N. (2019). | Are lucid dreams good for us? Are we asking the right question? A call for caution in lucid dream research. *Frontiers in Neuroscience*, 13(1423), 1–4.

Solms, M. (2000). Dreaming and REM sleep are controlled by different brain mechanisms. *Behavioral & Brain Sciences*, 23(6), 793–1121.

Sterpenich, V., Perogamvros, L., Tononi, G., & Schwartz, S. (2020). Fear in dreams and in wakefulness: Evidence for day/night affective homeostasis. *Human Brain Mapping*, 41(3), 840–850.

Stumbrys, T., & Erlacher, D. (2014). The science of lucid dream induction. In R. Hurd & K. Bulkeley (Eds.), *Lucid Dreaming: New Perspectives on Consciousness in Sleep* (pp. 77–102). CA: Praeger.

Tennyson, A. (2013). *The Complete Works of Alfred, Lord Tennyson*. Delphi Classics.

Vallat, R., Chatard, B., Blagrove, M., & Ruby, P. (2017). Characteristics of the memory sources of dreams: A new version of the content-matching paradigm to take mundane and remote memories into account. *PLOS ONE*, 12(10), e0185262.

Vallat, R., & Ruby, P. M. (2019). Is it a good idea to cultivate lucid dreaming? *Frontiers in Psychology*, 10(2585), 1–4.

Van der Kolk, B. (2015). *The Body Keeps the Score: Mind, Brain and Body in the Transformation of Trauma*. Penguin.

Waggoner, R. (2014). Learning the depths of lucid dreaming. In R. Hurd & K. Bulkeley, (Eds.), *Lucid Dreaming: New Perspectives on Consciousness in Sleep*. CA: Praeger.

Walker, M. P., & van der Helm, E. (2009). Overnight therapy? The role of sleep in emotional brain processing. *Psychological Bulletin*, 135(5), 731–748.

Wamsley, E. J., & Stickgold, R. (2019). Dreaming of a learning task is associated with enhanced memory consolidation: Replication in an overnight sleep study. *Journal of Sleep Research*, 28(1).

Wamsley, E. J., Tucker, M. A., Payne, J. D., Benavides, J. A., & Stickgold, R. (2010). Dreaming of a learning task is associated with enhanced sleep-dependent memory consolidation. *Current Biology*, 20, 850–855.

Watt, C., Ashley, N., Gillett, J., & Halewood, M. (2014). Psychological factors in precognitive dream experiences: The role of paranormal belief, selective recall, and propensity to find correspondences. *International Journal of Dream Research*, 7(1), 1–8.

Wilmer, H. A. (1996). The healing nightmare: War dreams of Vietnam veterans. In D. Barrett (Ed.), *Trauma and Dreams* (pp. 85–99). Cambridge, MA: Harvard University Press.

Zadra, A. (1996). Recurrent dreams: Their relation to life events. In D. Barrett (Ed.), *Trauma and Dreams* (pp. 231–267). Cambridge, MA: Harvard University Press.